Praise for *The H*

OTHER BOOKS BY JEZ BUTTERWORTH PUBLISHED BY TCG

THE HILLS OF
CALIFORNIA

THE HILLS OF CALIFORNIA

Jez Butterworth

THEATRE COMMUNICATIONS GROUP
NEW YORK
2025

The Hills of California is published by Theatre Communications Group, Inc.,
520 Eighth Avenue, 20th Floor, Suite 2000, New York, NY 10018-4156

This volume is published in arrangement with Nick Hern Books Limited,
The Glasshouse, 49a Goldhawk Road, London W12 8QP

TCG books are exclusively distributed to the book trade by Consortium Book
Sales and Distribution.

ISBN 978-1-63670-218-6 (paperback)

A catalog record for this book is available from the Library of Congress.

Cover design by SpotCo

First TCG Edition, February 2025

THE HILLS OF CALIFORNIA

The Hills of California was produced by Sonia Friedman Productions and Neal Street Productions and premiered at the Harold Pinter Theatre, London, on 27 January 2024. The cast (in order of appearance) was as follows:

JILLIAN	Helena Wilson
PENNY / BIDDY	Natasha Magigi
MR POTTS / JOE FOGG	Richard Lumsden
RUBY	Ophelia Lovibond
PATTY	Lucy Moran
TONY	Alfie Jackson
GLORIA	Leanne Best
BILL / MR HALLIWELL	Shaun Dooley
DENNIS / JACK LARKIN	Bryan Dick
VERONICA / JOAN	Laura Donnelly
YOUNG GLORIA	Nancy Allsop
YOUNG JILL	Nicola Turner
YOUNG RUBY	Sophia Ally
YOUNG JOAN	Lara McDonnell
MR SMITH	Will Barratt
MRS SMITH	Georgina Hellier
LUTHER ST JOHN	Corey Johnson
DR ROSE	Stevie Raine

Director	Sam Mendes
Designer	Rob Howell
Lighting Designer	Natasha Chivers
Composer, Sound Designer & Arranger	Nick Powell
Choreographer	Ellen Kane
Musical Supervisor & Arranger	Candida Caldicot
Casting Director	Amy Ball CDG
Young Persons' Casting Director	Verity Naughton CDG

The Hills of California opened on Broadway at the Broadhurst
Theatre on September 29, 2024. It was produced by Sonia
Friedman Productions, No Guarantees Productions, Neal Street
Productions, Brian Spector, Sand & Snow Entertainment,
Stephanie P. McClelland, Barry Diller, Reade St. Productions,
Van Dean, Andrew Paradis/We R Broadway Artists Alliance,
Patty Baker, Wendy Bingham Cox, Bob Boyett, Butcher
Brothers, Caitlin Clements, Kallish Weinstein Creative, Michael
Scott, Steven Toll & Randy Jones Toll, City Cowboy Produc-
tions/Jamie deRoy, JKVL Productions/Padgett Ross Produc-
tions, Koenigsberg Riley/Tulchin Bartner Productions, Todd B.
Rubin/Carlos Medina, Silly Bears Productions/Omara Produc-
tions, Michael Wolk/Cali e Amici, in association with Manhat-
tan Theatre Club (Lynne Meadow, Artistic Director; Chris
Jennings, Executive Director). It was directed by Sam Mendes.
The designer was Rob Howell; the lighting design was by
Natasha Chivers; the composer/sound designer and arranger
was Nick Powell; the production stage manager was Charles M.
Turner III. The cast was:

JILLIAN	Helena Wilson
PENNY / BIDDY	Ta'Rea Campbell
MR POTTS / JOE FOGG	Richard Lumsden
RUBY	Ophelia Lovibond
PATTY / YOUNG GLORIA	Nancy Allsop
TONY	Liam Bixby
GLORIA	Leanne Best
BILL / MR HALLIWELL	Richard Short
DENNIS / JACK LARKIN	Bryan Dick
VERONICA	Laura Donnelly
YOUNG JILLIAN	Nicola Turner
YOUNG RUBY	Sophia Ally
YOUNG JOAN	Lara McDonnell
MR SMITH	Max Roll
MRS SMITH	Ellyn Heald
LUTHER ST JOHN	David Wilson Barnes
JOAN	Laura Donnelly
DR ROSE	Cameron Scoggins

For Belinda Stewart-Wilson

Characters

JILLIAN, *thirties*
PENNY, *a nurse, forties*
MR POTTS, *a piano tuner, fifties*
RUBY, *thirties*
PATTY, *thirteen*
TONY, *fourteen*
GLORIA, *thirties*
BILL, *forties*
DENNIS, *forties*
JOAN, *late thirties*

VERONICA, *late thirties*
YOUNG JILLIAN, *twelve*
YOUNG RUBY, *thirteen*
YOUNG GLORIA, *fourteen*
YOUNG JOAN, *fifteen*
JOE FOGG, *a lodger, fifties*
BIDDY, *a maid, fifties*
MR SMITH, *a guest, forty*
MRS SMITH, *a guest, thirty*
MR HALLIWELL, *a lodger, forty*
JACK LARKIN, *a performer, thirties–forties*
LUTHER ST JOHN, *a show-business manager, forties*
DR ROSE

Setting

A guest house, on the outskirts of Blackpool, an English seaside resort on the Irish Sea, in the late spring of 1955, and the summer of 1976.

ACT ONE

Seagulls. An ice-cream van playing 'I'm Popeye the Sailor Man'. A piano being tuned.

The public parlour of a Victorian guest house, on the edge of Blackpool, August 1976.

A few years into disuse. Four separate Formica tables. A tiki bar festooned in postcards, foreign currency, old crates, soda siphons. A KP Nuts calendar for 1973. Elsewhere, a Lucky Lady one-armed bandit. An old jukebox.

Stairs up, to the floors above. A doorway to the back kitchen. (It is from here, unseen, that the piano is being tuned.)

Enter JILLIAN, *from upstairs, carrying an old wicker crib, filled with junk. Photograph albums. Sheet music. A couple of pairs of children's tap shoes. An old ukulele.*

She drops it on a table. Lights a cigarette.

She starts to look through some of the photographs. Suddenly –

Someone is coming down the stairs. She stubs it out. Sprays air freshener. A beat.

JILLIAN. Mother?

    Enter PENNY, *a nurse, from upstairs, in uniform.*

PENNY. She's sleeping.

JILLIAN. Is she on her left or her right side?

PENNY. Her back.

JILLIAN. Her feet are purple.

PENNY. It's normal.

JILLIAN. Normal?

9

PENNY. When they haven't been up and about.

Beat. The piano.

JILLIAN. I'm Jill by the way.

PENNY. Penny.

JILLIAN. Where's Alice?

PENNY. Scarborough. For the weekend. Her anniversary.

JILLIAN. Right. Well, I'll show you around.

PENNY. There's no need.

JILLIAN. Nonsense.

PENNY. Honest. I've got my bearings.

JILLIAN. Nonsense.

PENNY. Really it's fine.

JILLIAN. Let me show you.

PENNY. You showed me yesterday.

Beat.

Sit down.

JILLIAN. I'm fine.

A beat. She sits. PENNY *takes out a blood-pressure monitor.*

PENNY. I'm just going to check your blood pressure. You pop it on your arm. Like so.

PENNY *puts it on* JILLIAN*'s arm. She pumps it up.*

Now just relax.

She begins to take JILLIAN*'s blood pressure.*

This house. It's called 'Seaview'.

JILLIAN (*distracted*). Hmm?

PENNY. The Seaview Hotel.

JILLIAN. Aye.

PENNY. It's just… I've looked out of every window, and you can't.

Beat.

You can't see the sea. Even on the top floor. You can see the car park. The bingo. If you lean right out you can see the Tower –

JILLIAN. I believe they call it poetic licence.

Beat.

Anyway, it's not the Seaview Hotel. It *was* the Seaview Guest House. Then the Seaview Luxury Guest House. Then the Seaview Luxury Guest House and Spa. Then the Seaview Luxury Guest House. The Seaview Guest House… Now it's just Seaview.

PENNY. Sounds like this house has been on quite a journey.

Beat. The piano.

JILLIAN. May I ask a question? My sister Joan. The one in America.

PENNY. California.

JILLIAN. Exactly. (*Stops.*) Wait. How –

PENNY. You told me. Yesterday.

Beat.

JILLIAN. Right. Well. She's stuck. In California. Her aeroplane was cancelled. Or postponed. Anyroad, she won't arrive till tomorrow at the earliest.

PENNY. Oh yes…

JILLIAN. Joan's Mum's favourite. Not favourite.

Beat.

Mum always used to say, 'Gloria's Gran… You're your dad, Ruby's Ruby. But Joan is me.' I just need advice. Not advice. Your opinion. You've been here before.

PENNY. If you're asking me what I think you're asking me, the answer is I don't know.

JILLIAN. Understood.

PENNY. It could be today. Could be tomorrow.

JILLIAN. Understood.

PENNY. How long's a piece of string?

JILLIAN. It's just Joan has to be here. It's imperative.

PENNY. All I know –

JILLIAN. You don't understand. I promised Mum. I promised her Joan would be here.

PENNY. All I can tell you… It's in God's hands now. But I'll say this. I've seen miracles before.

The piano bursts into a brief passage of a sonata. Stops on a flat note.

Hello. We're making progress…! Do you play?

JILLIAN. Me? No fear. Mother used to, but not for years.

PENNY. Then who plays?

Beat.

JILLIAN. Joan. Joan plays.

PENNY *reads the pressure dial. Removes the stethoscope.*

PENNY. Your blood pressure is high. Do you smoke?

JILLIAN. Me? No.

PENNY. Have you ever smoked?

JILLIAN. Never. Filthy habit. Mother won't abide it.

PENNY. Are you on any medication?

JILLIAN. Ventolin for my asthma. Betnovate for my eczema. Pepto-Bismol.

PENNY. Personal question. Are you on the pill?

JILLIAN. No.

PENNY. Are you pregnant?

JILLIAN. No fear.

PENNY. Planning to get pregnant?

Silence. JILLIAN *begins to sob.*

I'm sorry.

The piano. Children's voices, and JILLIAN's *attempt to control her sobs.*

Beat.

Here.

PENNY *hands her –*

JILLIAN. What's this?

PENNY. It's a leaflet.

JILLIAN (*reading*). 'The Process of Bereavement.'

PENNY. Don't read it now, but you might want to pop it somewhere safe.

JILLIAN *looks at the leaflet for a long time. Then at* PENNY. *A beat.*

JILLIAN. I'll pop it somewhere safe.

Silence.

PENNY. I didn't tell you this. Moreover, if anyone asks I will flat deny it.

JILLIAN. Sorry, what –

PENNY. You're right. I have been here before. At this stage. And at this point. This juncture. There's things they can do.

JILLIAN. Who?

PENNY. Dr Groves. Or failing that, Dr Onions.When the time comes. If you feel she has suffered enough. If you call him… Then Dr Groves, or failing that, Dr Onions… Dr Onions calls Dr Rose. And Dr Rose comes. Ups the morphine dose. And your mother drifts peacefully to heaven.

Beat.

JILLIAN. I see.

Beat.

Or... Dr Groves or Dr Onions calls Dr Rose, Dr Rose comes over. Ups the dose. And my mother drifts peacefully to hell.

Beat.

I'm just saying. If you buy all that. If you do then it stands to reason some people go to. Not just Adolf Hitler and Evel Knievel. Normal folk. Folk from Blackpool who've raised four girls alone. If they didn't find time to go to church and worship God, the same God what torpedoed their husband's destroyer. Then – (*Stops.*) My point is. Any minute now, Mum could be travelling from ninety-one Penny Avenue, Blackpool F-Y-five-one-D-U, from a life of misery and suffering, to *actual* hell. In which case –

PENNY *stands.*

Wait. Where are you going?

PENNY. Home. My shift is finished.

JILLIAN. But –

PENNY. I'll be back this evening to give her her salts.

PENNY *writes down something on her pad.*

JILLIAN. What's that?

PENNY. A telephone number. Dr Groves. Or failing that... (*Tears it off.*) Dr Onions.

She hands it to her.

Discuss it with your sisters. And in the meantime. Get some rest.

Pause.

I'm a mother too, Miss Webb. Six boys. And I'll let you into a secret. Mothers don't have favourites. We love you all the same.

Exit PENNY.

JILLIAN *puts the number in the leaflet, folds the leaflet, puts it in her pocket. The piano tuning stops. From offstage we hear* MR POTTS *close the lid of the piano.*

MR POTTS (*offstage*). Right. Done all I can.

Enter MR POTTS, *the piano tuner.*

POTTS. Well. It's hopeless. If I've said it once, a piano must be played. Blackpool. Morecombe. Fleetwood. It's the sea air. Wood is porous. Salt. Damp. Neglect. Plus time. And here we are. Noisy pedals. Sticky keys. Your Chappell can stand it. But your Broadwood piano, Challen, Stack and Walmer? Your Broadwood is like a horse. Neglect it, it gets jumpy. Take me. A hundred lunges per day. Physical jerks. Keeps the sap up. The cable tight. Turn your back for a couple of winters? What have you got? Squeaks. Buzzes. Rattles. Worn felt. Mouse droppings.

JILLIAN. Will it play?

POTTS. What? Oh it'll play. If they've had a drink. But you left it too long. By the way, how's your mother? The nurse says she's dying.

JILLIAN (*flat*). Did she.

POTTS. Aye, so she said. Up there, at death's door. Chances are she won't last the night. If you ask me it's the drought. Wireless says there's twenty-one-point-nought-seven per cent more deaths than 1975. Up in town it's all 'Kiss-Me-Quick Mine's a Choc-Ice'. Out here in the backstreets, carnage. Folk melting in their front rooms. There's an Old Folk's Home over Kirkham, they've left one poor sod in a conservatory, his blood boiled. Honest to God, his face melted. Ambulance. Morgue. Cemetery. Do Not Pass Go Do Not Collect Two Hundred Pound. That said, the nurse told me your mother has stomach cancer. In that case the drought's less of a factor. Because – let's face it – at the end of the day – cancer's cancer, in't it? Come rain or shine.

JILLIAN. Thank you for coming, Mr Potts. How will I pay you?

POTTS. You know I remember her. Your mother. From back in the day. Veronica Webb. She stuck out. On Pleasure Beach. Funfair. Woolworths. That black mane.

JILLIAN. It were chestnut.

POTTS. I danced with her once in the Ballroom. Christmas, 1953. She wore a crimson and cream polka-dot halterneck, stilettos, and red lipstick. Next day, Bank Holiday. She were top of Tower, pencil skirt, fishnets, holding hands with a sailor. Cripes, she was a looker. Those pins. I'd try not to stare.

JILLIAN. Well they're purple now.

POTTS. Tell me, Miss Webb. Your father. Was he a sailor?

JILLIAN. No, Mr Potts. He was the Boogie Woogie Bugle Boy from Company B.

POTTS. That's the spirit! I was looking at you just now. 'She's pulling my leg. Can she really be the daughter of that goddess?' But then hey Preston, there we are. That same cheeky mouth. Miss Cheeky Chops. Can I call you Miss Cheeky Chops?

JILLIAN. No.

Enter RUBY.

POTTS (*turning*). Hello. What have we here?

RUBY. Who's this? Who are you?

JILLIAN. This is Mr Potts. Mr Potts, this is my sister Ruby.

POTTS. Now this looks more like her. The lips. The hips. (*Behind his hand.*) The thrup'ny bits! Now we're getting warmer!

RUBY. Are you the twerp's been making a racket all morning?

POTTS. And we're off! Miss Cheeky Chops the Second! Don't mind me. I like a woman with a tongue!

RUBY. What the fuck is he on about?

JILLIAN. Ruby –

RUBY. Mr –

POTTS. Potts.

RUBY. Mr Potts. Tell me. Have you completed your task?

POTTS. I've made the best of a bad job. I were just saying –

RUBY (*interrupting*). That's splendid. Do me a favour would you? Give the door a good slam on the way out.

Beat.

POTTS. So. Cash, cheque or postal order. No rush. But it's too late. Salt. Damp. Neglect. Plus time. If I've said it once, a piano must be played.

Exit MR POTTS.

RUBY *heads behind the bar, passing the jukebox.*

RUBY. What's that?

JILLIAN. What's it look like?

RUBY. How long's it been there?

JILLIAN. Since about 1960.

RUBY. What's it doing there?

JILLIAN. Nowt. It's been broke for years.

RUBY. When's this from? 1942?

She picks up a half-full bottle of gin.

JILLIAN. It's gin. Gin lasts for ever.

RUBY. Thank Christ something does.

JILLIAN *watches her pour.*

JILLIAN. Is Dennis awake?

RUBY. Search me. He didn't make it home last night.

JILLIAN. What happened?

RUBY. We were in The Galleon. Dennis had a row with the barman. A Welshman.

JILLIAN. Rhys.

RUBY. One minute they're singing songs, Dennis going on about his auntie in Wrexham, the next they're having a row. Dennis called…

JILLIAN. …Rhys.

RUBY. Rhys… Dennis called Rhys a Welsh cunt. Rhys threw us out. Then *we* had a row, on the seafront. Dennis stormed off. Or I stormed off. The last thing he said was 'I'm going for a swim.' Either that or 'I'm going back to Rochdale.' Hard to say. With the wind. Plus he was very, very drunk.

JILLIAN. So your husband is either in Rochdale, or drowned.

RUBY. What did the nurse say?

JILLIAN. Same. I went in this morning. Rubbed her feet. They're purple.

Beat.

Have you been in?

RUBY. I popped my head in.

JILLIAN. Did you talk to her?

RUBY. Give me a chance. I just got here.

Beat.

Is that a wig?

JILLIAN. From Beauty Spot.

RUBY. It looks terrifying.

JILLIAN. It cost twenty pound.

RUBY. She looks like a ghost.

JILLIAN. It's real hair.

Beat.

RUBY. Well I don't believe you. Mum wouldn't have any of this rubbish in her parlour.

JILLIAN. She wanted to attract a younger crowd. Spent a whole season's profits on boxes of badges. Balloons. Leaflets. She had an ad at the Odeon. Starring Mum, in a miniskirt, with me, sweet sixteen, tap shoes, singing this daft jingle. Mum with her posh voice –

RUBY. Oh no.

JILLIAN. 'Just two minutes from this cinema! Now with its own jukebox!'

RUBY. Two minutes?! It's four tram stops!

JILLIAN. Anyroad, it didn't work. Half those boxes are still up there in the attic.

RUBY. Well good luck with that. Only folk stopped here were too broke or tight to stop in town. Alkies, swindlers, the lost. Two-bob Don Juans on a spree. Who wants pop blaring while you're upstairs trying to shag your secretary? Have nervous breakdown. And by the way you're wrong. Nothing lasts for ever. This tastes like donkey piss.

Enter PATTY, *a girl, thirteen.*

Who the fuck are you?

JILLIAN. Cripes. Patricia. Is that you?

Enter TONY, *a boy, fourteen.*

Good gracious me. Is that Anthony?

TONY. No.

JILLIAN. Come on, Anthony. You can't fool me.

TONY. It's not. It's not Anthony.

PATTY. He's Tony now.

JILLIAN. Oh!

RUBY. Tony.

JILLIAN. Hello, Tony.

TONY. Hello, Aunt Jill.

RUBY. Where's Mum and Dad.

TONY. Outside. Rowing with the meter maid.

JILLIAN. Patty and Tony. All grown up.

PATTY. Bony Tony.

TONY. Piss off.

PATTY. Sorry. (*Under her breath.*) Bony Tony.

TONY. Say that again.

PATTY. Say what? Bony Tony?

TONY *flies at* PATTY *and* PATTY *gets him in a headlock.*

RUBY. Wow. That escalated fast.

Enter GLORIA, *followed by* BILL, *carrying bags.*

GLORIA. YOU TWO. PACK IT IN NOW. I SAID STOP.

She smacks both of them. Hard. It's violent.

I'M NOT GONNA SPEND THE NEXT FEW DAYS
REFEREEING SOME FIFTH-RATE WRESTLING
MATCH. NOW GIVE OVER, THE PAIR OF YOU.

TONY. Sorry, Mum.

GLORIA *slaps them both a couple more times and gives*
TONY *a knee in the thigh for good measure. Both kids end*
up on the floor.

Beat.

GLORIA. What the hell's going on, Jillian?

JILLIAN. Wh–

GLORIA. There's parking meters all the way from seafront to
Talbot Road! We've come two hundred miles across the
Gobi Desert, fucking Lawrence of Arabia, and we get here
and missus is waiting in her stupid hat telling me to park in
Acre Gate!

BILL. She's just hot and bothered. Aren't you, pet?

He tries to hug her.

GLORIA. For God's sake, Bill. Did you brush your teeth this morning? You've got bog breath. I'm four feet away. It's like a ray-gun.

BILL. I brushed them sixty. And I rolled on.

GLORIA. What the fuck's that?

The jukebox. BILL *puts on a 'scientist voice'.*

BILL. I'm no expert but it looks like one of those modern automated record-playing –

GLORIA. Can I stop you there? What did we talk about? What did we talk about in the car?

BILL. I'm sorry.

GLORIA. Are you going to do your voices? Just tell me now. Are you going to do your daft voices. Because I swear to God.

BILL. I'm not going to do my voices.

RUBY. It's a jukebox.

GLORIA. I know what it is. What's it doing in public parlour?

RUBY. Nowt. It's been broke for years.

GLORIA *looks for a brief moment like she is going to murder several of them. When she speaks, it's all business.*

GLORIA. Right. (*To the kids.*) You two. Pound each. Get up the pier.

PATTY. Where's the pier?

GLORIA. Where it always was. Or have they moved that 'n' all? Ont' sea, you daft bastards. Follow shitehawks. (*To* BILL.) You, get up Gowers. Baileys. Twiglets. Black Magic.

RUBY. And gin.

BILL. Shall I unpack first?

GLORIA. Do as you're told. And get yourself some Tic Tacs.

BILL. Baileys. Twiglets. Black Magic. Tic Tacs.

RUBY. And gin.

JILLIAN. Gowers is gone.

GLORIA. What?

RUBY. Gowers?

GLORIA. Where's it gone?

JILLIAN. It shut down. There's just the Co-op now.

Pause.

GLORIA. So now Gowers is gone…

Once again, everyone braces.

BILL. So –

JILLIAN. Left ont' corner. Right right left. Left again. Right.

BILL. Got it. (*Stops.*) My mum always said get over the rough ground as lightly as possible.

He leaves.

JILLIAN. I'll make you a cup of tea.

She goes behind the bar.

RUBY. So. Gloria. Lovely to see you. I thought we weren't bringing children.

GLORIA. Before you say 'owt, I don't want 'em here either. Blame Joyce.

RUBY. Who's Joyce?

GLORIA. His sister. That woman gets good use out of a chair. I don't want them here, but they're here so give over.

Beat.

Well come on. How is she?

Beat.

JILLIAN. Well, the nurse says she's seen miracles before.

GLORIA. Have you seen her?

RUBY. I've popped my head in.

GLORIA. And?

JILLIAN. Basically, how long's a piece of string.

GLORIA. Is she talking?

JILLIAN. Bits and bobs.

GLORIA. Have you spoken to her?

RUBY. Give me a chance. I just got here.

> *Enter* DENNIS, *forties. Holding a '99' with a Flake. He has the look of a man who hasn't been to bed. Half his face is very sunburnt. He's missing a plimsoll and a sock.*

DENNIS (*singing to himself*).
King 'Enry the Eighth had several wives
Including Anne Boleyn

> *Then:*

Morning, all!

JILLIAN. Dennis.

RUBY. Dennis, dear. You're back.

DENNIS. Morning, darling. Ravishing as always. Morning, Jill. Crumbs. Is that Gloria? I simply don't know how you do it, Gloria. Ten years. Is it voodoo? Flash bang wallop. What a picture. Your Bill's a lucky fella waking up to that each morning. Is he here?

RUBY. Aye. And the children.

> *Beat.*

DENNIS. Splendid.

RUBY. Bill's gone up the Co-op. Why don't you pop after him? Give him hand.

DENNIS. To be honest I quite fancy a sit-down. It's quite a stroll from the Golden Mile. Plus it's baking out.

Beat.

Um tiddly um pum pum pum pum.

Beat.

Do you know what, though? I'd love to see the Co-op. Can I have a glass of water first?

RUBY. No.

DENNIS. Splendid. So out the door –

JILLIAN. Left at the corner. Right right left. Left again. Right –

DENNIS. Right. Well I'm off to catch Bill. And you know what? I'm excited. I am. I'm raring to get back out there. Never waste a sunny day. That's what I always say.

He leaves.

(*Singing.*) Clap 'ands, stamp yer feet
Bangin' on the big bass drum

Exit DENNIS.

RUBY. Do you know, Dennis was born on the exact same day as Marlon Brando. And there, the similarity came to a shuddering halt.

GLORIA *stands.*

GLORIA. Right.

She goes out, and up the stairs. Silence.

RUBY. Well I simply can't believe it.

JILLIAN. Believe what?

RUBY. Gowers. I can't believe it's gone. Gowers is Gowers. You get off the tram. Gowers. What happened, Jillian?

JILLIAN (*distracted*). What? When?

RUBY. To Gowers.

JILLIAN. Gowers shut ten years back. Mr Gower died. Mrs Gower slogged on for a few years. Then she died.

RUBY. Well that explains it.

Re-enter GLORIA. RUBY *pours her sister a gin. Hands it to her. She drinks it. A beat.*

GLORIA. Is that a wig?

Beat.

JILLIAN. From Beauty Spot.

Beat.

RUBY. It's real hair.

Silence. RUBY *fills her glass again.*

JILLIAN. So yes. Gowers is gone.

Pause.

You know Owen Owen's in Hall Street that was. And then it changed to Purvis's. That shut last week. Windows all whitewashed. You just stand there in amazement.

Silence. GLORIA *stares ahead.*

Bingo's still there. Mum used to go.

RUBY. Mum went to bingo?

JILLIAN. Mmmm? Oh aye. Lots.

RUBY. *Our* mum?!

Both JILLIAN *and* RUBY *seem relieved to have found a subject with some life in it.*

JILLIAN. Tuesdays and Fridays. For years. Tram into town, best togs, up Tricia's for a shampoo and set, manicure, Campari in The George, back up bingo. She won a hundred pound once.

RUBY. Mum used to laugh at bingoers. 'Shoot me first,' she said.

JILLIAN. Well she went. And she won. A sun lamp. A salad bowl and servers. A floral encasement. A day trip to Scotney Castle. Front-row seats to Ken Dodd at The Grand. And dinner after with the man himself.

RUBY. Tea with Ken Dodd?

JILLIAN. At Lobster Pot. Him and his agent.

RUBY. What was he like?

JILLIAN. Oh she never went.

RUBY. Why not?

JILLIAN. 'Cause she's Mum.

RUBY. Why didn't you go?

JILLIAN. No fear.

RUBY. What about bingo?

JILLIAN. What?

RUBY. Bingo. Did you go?

JILLIAN. I stopped here, mind the fort.

RUBY. Mum at bingo. And tea at Lobster Pot. With Ken Dodd.

JILLIAN. Aye. There's lots gone on.

RUBY *and* JILLIAN *seem satisfied to have explored this.*

GLORIA. Ask me it's a bloody miracle.

RUBY. Y'what?

GLORIA. I say it's a miracle they let her in. A salad bowl and servers. Floral encasement. Sat here like three pillocks. If Mum went up the bingo, it were for the same reason she ever set foot in The Trades and Labour, The Brunswick. Why? Because the bar stays open all day. You can sit there, get pickled and no bugger bats. 'Rise and shine, twenty-nine'… 'Same again, love. Slip a brandy in it.'

JILLIAN. That's not fair.

GLORIA. If Mum were catching tram in her hoochie-boots, having manicures and tea at Lobster Pot with Ken Dodd, then why did I get a letter six months back from her at number ninety-five saying Mum were out in the street in her bra at four in the morning. That there was more bottles by her back bins than round the back of the Legion? She weren't allowed int' Co-op. She stunk like a skip. You can stick a cherry on it with all the sun lamps and salad bowls in the world. That person up there is dying. Now there's a job to be done, let's get it done, and get. Ruby?

RUBY. Roger.

GLORIA. Jillian.

JILLIAN. She wasn't in her bra.

GLORIA. I've got the bloody letter!

JILLIAN. She wasn't in her bra!

Silence.

GLORIA. So where is she? Where's our famous sister?

Beat.

JILLIAN. Her aeroplane was cancelled. Or postponed.

GLORIA. Well which is it?

JILLIAN. She said she was coming. If Joan says –

GLORIA. Then where is she?

JILLIAN. If Joan says she's coming, she's coming.

GLORIA. Well keep an eye out that window. If you see a stretch limo. Or helicopter. Shall we put bunting up?

JILLIAN. That's not very nice.

GLORIA. I'm here. Ruby's here.

JILLIAN. All right –

GLORIA. Times like these you find out who a body is. But go on. Stick up for her.

JILLIAN. I'm not sticking up for her.

GLORIA (*to* RUBY). See? (*Under her breath.*) Head in the clouds!

JILLIAN. Stop it.

GLORIA. It were like a fucking oven in that car! Nine hours. I've sweat clean through my slacks. (*To* RUBY.) How long did it take you and Dennis? From Rochdale?

RUBY. Not that long, as it happens. And the Datsun's got air-conditioning.

GLORIA *laughs.*

What?

GLORIA. Thank you. Thanks for the support.

RUBY. What? It has.

GLORIA. What did we say on the phone? What did we agree? On the phone, yesterday. What did you say you'd do?

RUBY. I'm sorry, Gloria, but I fail to see how the Datsun having air-cond–

GLORIA. See?

RUBY. It fucking does!

GLORIA. No go on. You're grand. Just… thanks for the backup. Thanks. It's nice to know who you can trust.

Beat.

JILLIAN. Well I'm sorry. But it's not Silly Jilly Head-in-the-Clouds, nor sticking up for no one. I know my sister. If Joan says she's coming, she's coming. There. I've said it.

Silence.

GLORIA. Well she better get a move on. That's all I'll say.

Silence.

JILLIAN. Is it nice?

RUBY. Is what nice?

JILLIAN. Air-conditioning.

> RUBY *gives a small shake of her head, 'Best not go there.'*
> *Silence.*

> GLORIA *suddenly sobs.*

Oh. Gloria.

RUBY. Glor, give over.

> JILLIAN *approaches.*

GLORIA. Don't touch me…

> JILLIAN *reaches out to console her.*

(*Bellows.*) DO NOT TOUCH ME! NOBODY TOUCH ME!

> *Silence.*

> JILLIAN *looks at her sisters. She closes her eyes.*

JILLIAN (*singing*).
The Seaview Luxury Guest House and Spa
Just around the corner from this cinema
Turn left at the Tower, a hundred yards approx
With colour television and our own jukebox!

> *As she sings, she tap-dances a little. At the end she strikes*
> *a pose and beams.*

> RUBY *laughs like a drain.* GLORIA *doesn't.* RUBY *springs*
> *up.*

RUBY. That's magic! Do it again.

JILLIAN (*singing*).
The Seaview Luxury Guest House and Spa
Just around the corner from this cinema
Turn left at the Tower, a hundred yards approx
With colour television and our own jukebox!

RUBY. Show me!

RUBY *falls into step.*

JILLIAN *and* RUBY (*singing*).
The Seaview Luxury Guest House and Spa
Just around the corner from this cinema
Turn left at the Tower, a hundred yards approx
With colour television and our own jukebox!

GLORIA (*over their singing*). All right. That's enough. All
right. Enough. Pack it in.

*The sisters keep going. And together they perform the jingle,
with the steps, faster.*

JILLIAN *and* RUBY (*singing*).
The Seaview Luxury Guest House and Spa
Just around the corner from this cinema
Turn left at the Tower, a hundred yards approx
With colour television and our own jukebox!

GLORIA (*over their singing*). I SAID PACK IT IN. NOW!
STOP IT. BLOODY STOP IT. I'M WARNING YOU. STOP
IT NOW!

…Until the two sisters collapse in a heap, giggling.

*Suddenly. From upstairs. They hear a cry. A haunting bellow
that shakes the house. It sounds like:*

VOICE. JOAAAN!!

RUBY *and* JILLIAN *both sit bolt upright. All freeze, then,
as one, the two sisters run upstairs.*

GLORIA *sits there. Alone.*

Silence.

*From the kitchen, we hear children's voices. Shadows
moving. The voices carry through to* GLORIA, *who sits
motionless in the front parlour.*

CHILDREN'S VOICES (*singing*).
Packed my suitcase wrote a note
And left it on the porch swing –

GLORIA *sits very still.*

VERONICA. Gloria!

YOUNG GLORIA. Coming, Mum!

Enter YOUNG GLORIA, *fourteen, running down the stairs. She hurries into the front parlour.*

(*NB* GLORIA *doesn't look at* YOUNG GLORIA *or vice versa.*)

YOUNG GLORIA *searches behind the bar, under chairs, etc.*

GIRLS (*singing*).
I'm headed West to make these dreams of mine come true –

YOUNG GLORIA *spots the crib. She goes over, rummages and comes up with the ukulele.*

VERONICA. Gloria!

YOUNG GLORIA. I'm coming!

Holding the ukulele, she rushes out, down the hall, into the back kitchen.

Leaving older GLORIA *alone.*

In the back, the piano rolls... And the next moment we are in –

The back kitchen. Evening. May. 1955.

YOUNG RUBY *and* YOUNG JILLIAN *are around the piano.* YOUNG GLORIA *enters with her ukulele.* JOE FOGG *is on the piano.*

GIRLS (*singing*).
The hills of California are something to see!
The sun will kinda warm ya, then drop in the sea
Though we overworked terrific
The blue Pacific is all Balboa claimed that it would be!

VERONICA *is at the stove, cooking a fish-and-chip supper for everyone. She puts the chips on, and begins whisking the batter.*

The hills of California will give ya a start
I guess I better warn ya, 'cause you'll lose your heart

Enter YOUNG JOAN, *from outside.*

VERONICA *flicks her whisk once and everyone stops on a dime.*

YOUNG JOAN. Sorry I'm late. I… I lost track of time.

VERONICA *doesn't acknowledge* YOUNG JOAN. *She takes a tea towel, wipes her hands, and turns to* YOUNG JILLIAN.

VERONICA. Jillian.

Beat. YOUNG JILLIAN *steps forward.*

YOUNG JILLIAN *(singing)*.

I guess I better warn ya! 'Cause you'll lose your heart!

Outside the room, we see BIDDY, *in a pinafore, showing some guests into the parlour.*

BIDDY. This way please…

VERONICA. Ruby.

YOUNG RUBY *steps forward. Sings the line.*

Gloria.

YOUNG GLORIA *sings it. A bit flat at the end.*

Together.

They all sing the line together.

Enter BIDDY, *from the hall. She knocks lightly on the frame of the door.*

BIDDY. Mrs Webb.

VERONICA. I'll be right there, Biddy. Gloria. We've been over this a million times.

BIDDY. It's just there's a gentleman here.

VERONICA. Thank you, Biddy. (*To* YOUNG GLORIA.) Gloria. You're wobbling on the half-note. Jillian. More voice on the chorus.

YOUNG JILLIAN. I'm wheezy.

VERONICA. Wheezy.

BIDDY. He's got a female with him. A young female. They don't appear to have any luggage.

VERONICA. Thank you, Biddy. Make them comfortable. I'll be with you presently.

The phone rings. She picks up the bowl and whisks her way back past YOUNG JOAN *to the stove…*

Jillian. If Johnny Mercer had got halfway across 'The Hills of California' and thought, 'Cor, this is a slog, I'm feelin' a bit wheezy,' then Johnny Mercer wouldn't be Johnny Mercer. Your inhaler is in your cubby.

VERONICA *heads across to the phone.*

Good evening, Miss Joan. I see you've deigned to grace us with your presence.

YOUNG JOAN. I'm sorry I'm late –

Before YOUNG JOAN *can answer,* VERONICA *picks up the phone.*

VERONICA (*posh voice*). Seaview Luxury Guest House and Spa! Speaking. Tonight you say? Let me just have a look.

She covers the receiver.

We can do this the easy way or the hard way, Joan. You want to spend your nights at Funfair flirting with boys and end up grinding a mangle on Ribble Road with five kids, just keep it up, love. If not, get your arse in line.

YOUNG JOAN. Yes, Mum –

VERONICA (*into phone*). Hello, caller? It appears you're in luck. I've a twin on the top floor. It enjoys a basin and a lovely sea view. Can I have a – ? Mr Hurst. Six o'clock. I'll expect you then. Goodbye.

She hangs up.

Gloria, you're flat as a flan top of two. Ruby, stop dead on the second 'T' of 'start'. Straighten up. Eyes front chin up chest out three four.

The song starts that instant.

GIRLS (*singing*).
A buzzard took a monkey for a ride in the air
The monkey thought that everything was on the square
The buzzard tried to throw the monkey off of his back
But the monkey grabbed his neck and said 'Now listen, Jack'

Straighten up and fly right
Straighten up and fly right
Straighten up and fly right
Cool down, Papa, don't you blow your top
Ain't no use in divin'
What's the use of divin'
Straighten up and fly right
Cool down, Papa, don't you blow your top

As the GIRLS sing, VERONICA puts the fillets on a tray and carries chips and fillets to the table and plonks them on it. As they hit, the song ends, bang on the drop.

VERONICA. Put your puddings up for treacle.

SISTERS. Yes!

YOUNG GLORIA. I'm so hungry!

They all dive around for the table. In the melee, JOE takes a flask out of the top of the piano and takes a sly nip.

VERONICA. Joe Fogg, I've told you a hundred times. Please don't store your Scotch in the Broadwood. You spill a pint of Hankey Bannister's in her you'll be working till 1999 just to pay me back.

JOE. Sorry, Mrs Webb.

They all sit and fall on the food. (Throughout the following, JOE, variously: replaces a string on a ukulele, tunes it to the piano, and generally tinkers away.)

VERONICA. Girls. I have some bad news. The performance at the St Bartholomew's on Saturday has been cancelled.

YOUNG JILLIAN *and* YOUNG JOAN. No!

YOUNG GLORIA. What?

YOUNG RUBY. What happened, Mum?

VERONICA. It seems Father Troy has had a change of heart. After our performance at the village fete last June, some of the congregation got together and found your performance 'too raucous, crude and stimulating for a place of worship'. Now the Deacon of Lancashire has got involved and the Deacon of Lancashire has leant on Father Troy and Father Troy has folded like a deckchair. Says he doubled-booked with a baptism. Or a confirmation.

JOE. Or an exorcism?

JOE *plays a couple of bars of the theme from* The Mummy.

VERONICA. Now, Ruby. What is this?

YOUNG RUBY. An obstacle.

VERONICA. An obstacle. And who else in their careers –

Enter a man, MR HALLIWELL.

Good evening, Mr Halliwell. Can I help you?

HALLIWELL. Good evening, Mrs Webb. I'm just up to my room.

VERONICA. I see. Well in that case, Mr Halliwell, may I inform you, again, and for what is going to be the very final time, this is the private parlour. Through there is the public parlour. There is a door to Penny Avenue. That is the door you may use to gain access.

HALLIWELL. But, Mrs Webb, I work in Dover Street, I have to go down Carrisbrook, left on Horton Avenue, left again all way down the alley, left and up Penny Avenue. It takes me ten more minutes.

VERONICA. Nevertheless. Now off you trot.

HALLIWELL. But I'm here now.

He makes a move to get past her. She stands in his way. He makes a small move the other way. She moves too. Impasse.

VERONICA. I can clear this up for you. The next time you see fit to traipse clean through my kitchen and do the hokey-pokey while my girls are having supper, is the last time you set foot in the Seaview Luxury Guest House and Spa.

HALLIWELL. But it's ten more minutes!

VERONICA. I don't care if it's a week, or via Timbuktu. You stop here, you follow my rules. On your way now.

Pause.

HALLIWELL. Suffering Jesus…

He turns round and leaves.

VERONICA. Now then. Obstacles. Children, who else, in their career, when they were starting out, faced a barrage, nay avalanche of seemingly unsurmountable hurdles, hitches, snags, bars, blocks and impediments.

ALL. The Andrews Sisters.

VERONICA. The Andrews Sisters. Maxene. Patty and LaVerne Andrews.

JOE FOGG cues them on the ukelele.

ALL (*singing*).
    Drinkin' rum and Coca-Cola
    Go down Point Cumana
    Both mother and daughter
    Workin' for the Yankee dollaaaarrrrr!

They all whoop and laugh.

YOUNG GLORIA. Oh, beat it, man, beat it!

YOUNG RUBY. Oh, you vex me, you vex me!

BIDDY reappears in the doorway, worried.

BIDDY. Mrs Webb.

VERONICA. I'm coming, Biddy.

BIDDY. It's just that gentleman said he's –

VERONICA. I SAID I'M COMING!

Pause.

Hold that thought. Ruby, get your elbows off table. Gloria, leave some chips for the others. (*As she walks away.*) That lass can eat two more spuds than a pig.

She heads into the public parlour. We hear her greeting a gentleman.

Good evening, sir. Miss. How can I be of assistance?

At the table, YOUNG JOAN *holds the potato ladle like it's a microphone, and speaks in a fast accent.*

YOUNG JOAN (*American*). Here's a couple of kids over here who are going overseas to Europe and they are Maxene, Patty…

The others use American accents too.

YOUNG JILLIAN *and* YOUNG RUBY. Hi Tom!

YOUNG JOAN. And LaVerne.

YOUNG GLORIA. Hello Tom!

JOE *plays the Pathé News fanfare, then accompanies under…*

YOUNG JOAN. So you're all three sisters of course but which one of you started professionally singing and sort of led the way or did you all go on together?

YOUNG GLORIA. Well I think I did. I'm the eldest, Tom, and I played piano.

YOUNG JOAN. By the way, Maxene, I love the pin.

YOUNG RUBY. Thank you, Tom. See I want to become an individualist. Sure, I'm tired of being one of three.

They all imitate the interviewer's laugh.

YOUNG JOAN. It must be wonderful playing in front of a live audience. For instance you're going over to the Palladium. A real terrific thrill getting the reaction of the public instead of in... in cold studios or in movies and suchlike.

YOUNG JILLIAN. Yes it's a big thrill.

YOUNG RUBY. I don't think there's anything more exhilarating than working in front of a live audience.

YOUNG GLORIA. It's real exciting.

VERONICA. This way please.

YOUNG JOAN. Girls! I want to thank you but I hear the ship's horn a-blowin'. Have a wonderful time over in England and we'll be wishing you all the best.

ALL SISTERS. Thank you. / Thank you. / Thank you, Tom.

JOE. I tell ya where needs an exorcism! This place.

VERONICA *leads the guests up the stairs.*

VERONICA. Alabama, Colorado, Mississippi, Indiana, Massachusetts, Minnesota, Oklahoma, Tennessee and Alaska. You're in Alaska. It's on the top floor, turn left at the WC.

MR SMITH. Aye. Thank you.

MRS SMITH. Thank you.

VERONICA. Now there's one solid-gold rule and that's no and I mean strictly no smoking. Not in the room. The parlour. And don't crack a window and tab it out 'cause I'm part bloodhound.

MR SMITH. Understood.

VERONICA. Top floor turn left at the WC. Enjoy your stay, Mr and Mrs Smith.

Re-enter VERONICA.

So. The Andrews Sisters – Maxene, LaVerne and Patricia – faced many many obstacles. Jillian.

YOUNG JILLIAN. They were born into poverty in Minnesota.

VERONICA. Ruby.

YOUNG RUBY. They had to practise in the back of their father's Buick between shows.

YOUNG GLORIA. The shows were sometimes three hundred miles apart and when they got there the shows were –

VERONICA. The shows were sometimes cancelled. Because it was –

ALL. The Great Depression.

VERONICA. The Great Depression of 1929.

JOE plays the theme from The Grapes of Wrath.

An economic shock that impacted most countries across the world. Banks foreclosed on businesses. Factories. Farms. And –

ALL. Dance halls.

VERONICA. Halls would close overnight. The sisters would rehearse in that Buick for three hundred miles, arrive and be turned away. Jill, give me another obstacle.

YOUNG JILLIAN. They were hungry all the time.

VERONICA. Constantly starving. Gloria.

YOUNG GLORIA. They were very young.

VERONICA. Patty Andrews was seven years old when they started out. Another obstacle. Joan.

YOUNG JOAN. LaVerne Andrews was ugly as sin.

YOUNG GLORIA laughs. Long. No one else laughs. She stops.

VERONICA. In the corner please, Joan.

YOUNG JOAN. Yes, Mum.

She goes and sits in the corner.

VERONICA. And so, girls. The lesson we take from this hiccup is that the road ahead is a bumpy one. It's not for the fainthearted, the uncommitted, the weak or the wheezy.

Out in the hall, a man is tiptoeing towards the bottom stair.

But it is a road we will travel together. Jack Larkin, stop right there.

The man stops.

Enter JACK LARKIN.

ALL. Evening, Jack. / All right, Jack. / Evening, Mr Larkin. You all right.

JACK (*sombre*). Aye. I'm all right I suppose. It's just I just heard about these two nuns driving along when Count Dracula suddenly jumps onto their car. 'Quick, show him your cross.' The other nun shouts – (*Shouts loud.*) 'OI! DRACULA. HOP IT!!'

JOE punctuates the joke. Laughter. Groans.

A skeleton walks into a bar, says 'Can I have a pint of mild and a mop?'

As he tells his jokes, and JOE goes up the octaves, VERONICA dons oven gloves, and takes out a tray of muffins.

How do you kill a circus? Go for the juggler. Where do you find a cow with no legs? Right where you left it. What's orange and sounds like a parrot? *(They answer with him.)* A carrot.

They laugh.

Is it pity? Is it, madam?

YOUNG RUBY. Good day, Jack?

JACK. And a good day to you, missus. I've been busking over the train station. Get 'em while they're hot I say. Speaking of which.

VERONICA drops the tray of muffins on the table.

VERONICA. There's an oven bottom each. Get from under my feet. The Squadronaires Dance Orchestra are on the *Light Programme* in four minutes. Watch out, they're piping.

As they get up to leave, JOE *plays 'Boston Bounce' by The Squadronaires, and* JACK *quick-fires.*

JACK. Two cannibals are eating a clown. One says, 'Does this taste funny to you?'

YOUNG RUBY. Can I practise my scales, Mum?

VERONICA. I need a private word with Mr Larkin.

YOUNG RUBY. Please, Mum.

VERONICA *pulls out a pencil, with a rubber on the end.*

VERONICA. Practise ont' bar. Eighty-eight keys, rub it out when you're done. *Pianissimo.* There's paying guests through there.

JOE. Come along, Ruby, I'll help you with your scales.

As they head out, JACK *flits around them, seemingly unable to stop.*

JACK. A truck-load of tortoises crashed into a trainload of terrapins. Police are calling it a turtle disaster.

They all leave. (YOUNG JOAN *is still in the corner of the room.*)

My brother's got five cocks. His pants fit him like a glove.

VERONICA *doesn't laugh.*

Six hours I was down that station. Six trains from Liverpool, charabancs from Crosby, Formby. Birkenhead. Bootle. Half of Merseyside, and all they can spare is four bob and a bottletop. And they say Yorkshiremen are tight. Did you know a Scouse and a Yorkshireman once fought over a penny and that's how they invented copper wire?

VERONICA *stares levelly.*

Something wrong, Veronica? You seem mithered.

VERONICA. St Bartholomew's cancelled. They've had all year to get their knickers in a bunch. I've spent a month's profit on costumes, hairdressers. I've got a car booked to take us there. It's a ninety-seater church. It's smaller than Tabernacle!

Pause.

Anyway, it's put me behind, so I'll be needing that back-rent.

JACK *looks at her. Somehow he manages to shrink about a foot without seeming to move.*

JACK (*high Munchkin voice*). I'm afraid I'm a little bit short!

VERONICA. I don't mean to embarrass you, Jack, but that's exactly what you said and did last week. Stood right there or thereabouts. You were drunk then too. And it weren't funny then and it's not funny now. You're three months behind.

JACK. It a dry patch.

VERONICA. Aye, and the faster you turn it the quicker it goes round.

JACK. Mersey Week's a bugger. That Liverpool mob are tighter than an otter's pocket.

VERONICA. So this is their fault. / The Scousers.

JACK (*overlapping*). Ronnie! Ronnie Ronnie Ronnie –

VERONICA (*seething*). Don't you fucking 'Ronnie' me, you soft 'ap'th. 'I know Jimmy Bairstow. I know Doris Day! Last week I was in The Alhambra with Al Martino telling him all about you.' 'Were you, Jack? In that case, forget the rent. You can just take my money and piss it up the wall.' You said Max Bygraves's manager promised next time he was in Blackpool he would come here, to this house, and audition my girls. That was ten months back. So where is he? Where's Mr Manager?

Pause.

'I know the body runs The Feldman. Him what books The Queen's. The North Pier by June. Mark my words. June, Veronica. Mark it on the calendar.' 'It's May the first, Jack.

Where's the phone calls? The contracts?' 'Oh look, it's Mersey Week.' Aye, and my girls learned 'Molly Malone'. 'The Rose of Tralee'. With all the steps. Why? Because you said you could get them on the lunchtime roster at The Palace. Now half the world's here, buying tickets, looking for fun, something special, something to remember. And they'll come and they'll go back home and not one of them will have heard word nor whisper of the Webb Sisters. Why? Because they're a mile out of town, stuck in this stinking kitchen, rotting.

Pause.

This act were better six months ago. It's going off the boil. It kills me to admit it. But if I can feel it they can feel it. In their little bones. They think I'm lying to them. Why? Because I *am*. I look in their eyes and I can see the fire going out. Now I will not sit back and watch their dreams die. Because that's what's happening. That's what's happening right now.

Pause.

You're living here on hot air and tick, Jack Larkin. I've had it. Give me three months' rent or get. I must have been crackers to listen to you.

Silence.

JACK. I see.

Pause.

Well… then you won't want to hear what I've got to say.

VERONICA. You know what, Jack. You're dead right there.

JACK. Suit yourself.

VERONICA. You know what? I will. I will suit myself.

JACK. Look, I know how much you want your lasses to prosper.

VERONICA. Don't make me come over there and –

Beat.

'Prosper'?! 'Prosper'?! You want 'prosper' go work in a bank. I want them to live. To soar. Not dragged down by St Bartholomew's, or you. Or anyone. My girls are the Webbs. And the Webbs aren't ten-a-penny. They only made one lot, and they're here! They're right here!

Pause.

JACK. So when you collared me just now, I was popping upstairs to wash, then coming down because I have news. Important news. Concerning your girls.

VERONICA. You're a bastard, Jack Larkin.

JACK. Fine. I'm a bastard. Two words. Mae Ray. It took Mae Ray three weeks to move from the Grand to the Palladium. Six months later, she's at Carnegie Hall... Ask me this. Who's Mae Ray's little boy's godfather? Knock knock. Who's there? Opportunity. Come in, Mr O, sit yourself down. Thank you I don't mind if I do.

VERONICA. Just spit it out, you bastard. I'm not playing games.

JACK. Someone wants to meet your girls.

Beat.

VERONICA. Who?

JACK. You wanna know? Meet me in Oklahoma in ten minutes.

His bow tie spins round. He beams.

VERONICA. Oh, Jack, you dunce. This is how it works. 'I've got something you want, love.' (*Flirtatious.*) 'Have you, sir?'

JACK. Veronica –

VERONICA. I've got you wrong. You have got about a thousand times more cheek than I thought you had. Like I'm desperate enough I'm gonna come upstairs and drop me knickers, bend over bed and let you –

JACK (*interrupting, chirping*). Aaaand I never get sick at sea! What up, George. Easy now!

Only now VERONICA *spots* YOUNG JOAN, *standing in the corner.*

VERONICA. Joan.

Pause.

JACK. A three-legged dog walks into a saloon: 'I'm looking for the man who shot my paw.'

Silence.

VERONICA. Mr Larkin. Thank you for bringing this to my attention. As I say, I will not be joining you in Oklahoma. I will however meet you outside Minnesota, where you will have precisely one minute to say what you have to say.

JACK. Minnesota.

VERONICA. *Outside* Minnesota. By the communal toilet.

JACK. I'll be wearing a red carnation.

JACK smiles. And jigs…

(*Singing.*) I'm Sparking Jack Larkin
From Bradford to Dorking
I'll have the aisles rocking
The young ladies talking
They say that I'm barking
I'm not I'm just larking
I'm Sparking Jack Larkin
The best of them aaalllll!

Exit JACK. *Silence.*

VERONICA. Turn round please, Joan.

She does.

I would like to discuss the last few minutes. Now I don't want you to say anything. I just want you to listen very carefully. Are you listening?

Silence.

Joan?

YOUNG JOAN. Sorry. You, it's just, you said you didn't want me to say anything.

VERONICA. Answer the question.

YOUNG JOAN. Yes.

VERONICA. Good. Now. When children eavesdrop, earwig, snoop or pry, then they hear things they don't understand and they put two and two together. My point is, anything you may have heard, or think you may have heard, in the most recent exchange between myself and Mr Larkin –

YOUNG JOAN. I didn't hear anything.

Beat.

VERONICA. Be that as it may, if you were to try to put two and two together, and repeat any of that to your sisters –

YOUNG JOAN. I didn't hear a thing.

VERONICA. I'm not stupid, Joan.

YOUNG JOAN. It's the truth. I was just over here. Daydreaming.

Beat.

VERONICA. Daydreaming.

YOUNG JOAN. Aye.

VERONICA. About what?

YOUNG JOAN. Johnny Jones. From number seventeen. I was thinking about his eyes. He has this squint, see, which makes him look dreamy, but sometimes like he's looking at the person next door, or over there, at a dog. He asked me to the Churchtown Hop Saturday, I swear to God I thought he was asking Bridey McNeil. And then I started thinking about his brother Bernard. Bernard has beautiful eyes, but he's nasty. And so I was thinking if you could take Bernard's eyes and put them in Johnny's head, then I might go to the Hop with him. But then I thought I can't go to the Hop anyway, because I haven't got half-a-crown. But if I had half-a-crown I could go.

Pause.

VERONICA. So you're short half-a-crown.

YOUNG JOAN. Aye.

VERONICA. I see. Are you blackmailing me, Joan?

YOUNG JOAN. I wouldn't call it blackmail. I'd call it more…
pulling your leg.

VERONICA *looks at her.*

VERONICA. Well, Joan. I agree Johnny Jones is a cross-eyed,
spotty rotter who's too short to dance with. But you can't go
swapping boys' eyes about to suit your purpose. Their mums
don't like it. And there'd be blood all over.

YOUNG JOAN *giggles behind her hand, thrilled.*

Come here.

She does.

I'm going to speak very plainly now. Are you listening?

YOUNG JOAN. Yes, Mum.

VERONICA. What does any song-and-dance troupe need?
Answer. Talent. But it also needs.

YOUNG JOAN. Discipline.

VERONICA. Talent and discipline. What it doesn't need is
a broken wheel. It appears the height of your ambition,
young lady, is making Gloria Webb wet her knickers. You
know she looks up to you. They all do. Well this is your last
chance. If it happens again I will not hesitate to remove you.
That's right. Because I will not stand back and have you
destroy your sisters' dreams. In a few years' time, you'll be
living in a manky box in Ribble Road, you'll switch on your
wireless. 'Ladies and gentlemen, live from the London
Palladium…' How are you going to feel then?

YOUNG JOAN. Bad, Mum.

VERONICA. Good. Because that's what's gonna happen. Also
you'll show your mother the respect she deserves. What are
you going to do?

YOUNG JOAN. Not kill my sisters' dreams.

VERONICA. And.

YOUNG JOAN. Show my mother the respect she deserves.

VERONICA. Here's half-a-crown.

She hands it to her.

Practise the counter-melody. When I come back down I want it note perfect.

VERONICA *heads off.*

YOUNG JOAN. Mum…

She stops. Beat.

St Bartholomew's can go to hell.

VERONICA *is suddenly deeply moved. She comes over and hugs her daughter, tightly.*

She recovers herself.

MR HALLIWELL *enters, and goes upstairs.*

Goodnight, Mr Halliwell.

HALLIWELL (*to himself*). …Flaming…

He heads up. VERONICA *looks at* YOUNG JOAN.

VERONICA. Counter-melody.

YOUNG JOAN. Note perfect.

VERONICA *heads upstairs.* YOUNG JOAN *stands in thought. A beat.*

Enter YOUNG GLORIA, *followed by the other two.*

YOUNG GLORIA. 'LaVerne Andrews is ugly as sin.' I nearly died.

YOUNG JILLIAN. Did you see Mum's face? Like the Rock of Gibraltar!

YOUNG GLORIA. I thought I was gonna piss myself.

YOUNG RUBY *takes the last oven bottom.*

YOUNG RUBY. So if you could marry James Dean, Johnny Mercer, or Mystery Man A, who would you choose?

YOUNG JILLIAN. Who's Mystery Man A?

YOUNG RUBY. Mystery Man A is a mystery. Dark and mysterious who might turn out to be better than James Dean or Johnny Mercer. *Or*, he might turn out to be a murderer. Gloria.

YOUNG GLORIA. Johnny Mercer. Wait. Jimmy Dean.

YOUNG RUBY. Jill?

YOUNG JILLIAN. I'm not sure.

YOUNG RUBY. Joan?

Unseen by the others, YOUNG JOAN *has lit a cigarette. Breathes out a cloud of smoke. Everybody stops.*

YOUNG GLORIA. What the fuck are you doing?

YOUNG RUBY. Joan. What the fuck?

YOUNG JILLIAN. Joan?

YOUNG JOAN. What does it look like?

YOUNG RUBY. Are you daft? Mum'll slaughter you.

YOUNG JILLIAN. Put it out.

YOUNG RUBY. Put it out, Joan.

YOUNG JILLIAN (*simultaneous*). Jesus Christ. Where did you get them?

YOUNG JOAN. Gowers.

YOUNG RUBY. Old Mr Gower sold you ciggies?

YOUNG JOAN. Who said I paid for 'em?

YOUNG GLORIA. Don't tell me you pinched 'em!

YOUNG RUBY. Jesus fucking Christ.

YOUNG JILLIAN. I don't believe this.

She blows a plume of smoke. They watch.

YOUNG RUBY. My God. You look amazing.

YOUNG JILLIAN. Where's the smoke going? Are you eating it?

YOUNG RUBY. She's smoking. My sister's smoking!

YOUNG JOAN. Fancy a drag, Rube?

YOUNG RUBY. Are you mad?

YOUNG JOAN. Jill?

YOUNG JILLIAN. No fear.

YOUNG JOAN. No. Suit yourselves.

YOUNG GLORIA. I will.

Beat.

YOUNG RUBY. Bollocks. You wouldn't dare.

YOUNG JILLIAN. Gloria!

YOUNG RUBY. You wouldn't.

Pause. YOUNG GLORIA *is nervous, but excited.*

YOUNG GLORIA. What you waiting for? Give us a puff.

YOUNG JOAN. You sure.

She hands the cigarette to YOUNG GLORIA.

YOUNG RUBY. Are you daft?

YOUNG JILLIAN. Mum'll smell it.

YOUNG RUBY. She'll go spare.

YOUNG JILLIAN. Spare? She'll skin ya!

YOUNG GLORIA (*softly*). Shut up.

YOUNG GLORIA*'s hand is shaking a little.* YOUNG JOAN *gives her the cigarette. Pause.*

What do I do?

YOUNG JOAN. Stick it in your gob. Suck. (*Breathes in.*) Blow.

Everyone watches.

YOUNG GLORIA *puts it in her mouth. She sucks. Inhales. And blows.*

You didn't cough.

YOUNG GLORIA. Am I supposed to?

YOUNG RUBY. Glor?

YOUNG JILLIAN. Glor?

YOUNG RUBY. She's gone white.

YOUNG JILLIAN. She's gonna puke.

YOUNG JOAN. You know what you are, Gloria Webb. Hip.

YOUNG RUBY. You what?

YOUNG JILLIAN. What's hip?

YOUNG JOAN. Hip is cool.

YOUNG RUBY. Says who?

YOUNG JOAN. John Lee Hooker.

YOUNG JILLIAN. Hip?

YOUNG JOAN. It's the opposite of square. John Lee's hip. Nat King Cole's hip. And so's Gloria. She's hip as fuck.

YOUNG GLORIA *glows.*

YOUNG JILLIAN. Gimme a puff!

Silence.

YOUNG JOAN *looks at them all. At the cigarette. Something passes over her. She gets up and leaves the table.*

YOUNG RUBY. Joan? Are you all right?

YOUNG GLORIA. Are you all right, Joan?

Pause.

YOUNG JOAN. Mum's not happy.

Pause.

YOUNG RUBY. What do you mean?

YOUNG GLORIA. Why's she not happy? What did she say?

YOUNG RUBY. Joan? What did she say?

YOUNG JOAN. Last night in her room. She was praying. She said all our names to God and asked for his help. And this morning, I saw her down here. She hadn't been to bed. She was sitting there, at table. She'd been crying. She pretended she wasn't. It was awful.

Pause.

I'm sorry I was late for practice. It won't happen again. I mean it. From now on, I'll always be on time. Whenever the three of you need me. I'll be there. I swear.

YOUNG JILLIAN. Mystery Man A. I want to marry Mystery Man A.

Someone coming downstairs.

YOUNG RUBY. She's coming.

YOUNG JILLIAN. Fuck. Hide.

YOUNG JILLIAN *and* YOUNG RUBY *run about waving their arms around. Enter* VERONICA.

YOUNG RUBY. Hello, Mum.

YOUNG JILLIAN. Hello, Mum.

Beat.

Everything okay?

VERONICA *looks at* YOUNG JILLIAN *as if tuning in from a very long way away. She goes over to the piano.*

VERONICA. Joan. Come here please.

She does.

Sit down.

YOUNG JOAN *sits on the floor at her feet.*

Come here, girls.

They come over, and sit at her feet.

Joan, I want to say sorry.

Pause.

You were just having a laugh and a laugh is sometimes what we need. We'd had a setback, but as we all know, it's merely a bump in the road.

YOUNG JILLIAN. Are you all right, Mum?

VERONICA. All of you. Close your eyes.

They do.

Have you closed them?

ALL. Aye. / Yes. / Yes, Mum.

Pause.

VERONICA. Now I have a question. Are you all listening?

ALL. Yes. / Aye. / Yes, Mum.

VERONICA. Good. Now.

Beat.

What is a song?

Beat.

YOUNG JILLIAN. A song is a dream.

VERONICA. And…

ALL. A place to be.

VERONICA. A song is a place to be.

She plays a melody on the piano.

Somewhere you can live. And in that place, there are no walls. No boundaries. No locks. No keys. You can go anywhere.

Beat.

I want you to picture yourself in a warm, high place. The Californian hills. A dry warm breeze blowing from the south, kicking up the dust upon the red scarred earth. No rain, but still the scent of jasmine wafts through the canyon. The warmth of the sun on your face. The sound of buzzards. What else.

YOUNG JILLIAN. Eagles.

VERONICA. Eagles.

YOUNG RUBY. Crickets.

YOUNG JOAN. The ocean.

VERONICA (*singing*).
The hills of California are something to see…

ALL (*singing*).
The sun will kind of warm ya, then drop in the sea…

VERONICA. There. Now listen, girls. Listen to the wonderful news I have to tell you.

End of Act One.

ACT TWO

The public parlour. 1976.

On the table, a bottle of gin, a bottle of Baileys and a box of Black Magic. A small fan is on at the bar.

The three sisters sit at separate tables.

JILLIAN *is restless…* GLORIA *is watching her, without actually looking at her.*

RUBY *is reading from the guestbook, glass of Baileys, eating the chocolates.*

RUBY (*reading*). 'Thirtieth June 1947. Mr and Mrs A. Timlin, Esquire. Thirty-two Buckingham Terrace. Edinburgh. "A most relaxing stay."'

Pause.

'Mr Lionel Thribb, librarian, nine-and-a-half Church Street, Lincoln. "The plug on the sink in Alabama is missing."'

Silence. JILLIAN *looks up the stairs.*

GLORIA. What you doing?

JILLIAN. Me? Nothing.

GLORIA. You've been staring up them stairs for –

JILLIAN. I'm keeping an ear out.

GLORIA. Well stop it. You're making me nervous.

Beat.

RUBY. 'July second. Mr and Mrs George Wilkins, Esquire, thirteen Cromwell Terrace. Cockermouth. "A very relaxing bank holiday. Thank you."'

JILLIAN *goes behind the bar, fetches the crib.*

55

Beat.

RUBY. 'July eighteenth. Mr Bartholomew Pearson. Twenty-five Phoenix Road, Preston… "Shithole."'

Beat.

Everyone's a critic.

JILLIAN starts rooting through the crib slightly too earnestly. She can feel GLORIA watching her like a hawk.

GLORIA. What's that?

JILLIAN. What's what?

GLORIA. That.

JILLIAN. Just some old junk. Bits and bobs. I found it in the attic.

GLORIA. What bits and bobs?

JILLIAN. Bric-a-brac. Keepsakes.

GLORIA. What's it doing there?

JILLIAN. I'm just having a root.

GLORIA. Why?

JILLIAN. Well if you must know, I'm looking for something.

GLORIA. What?

JILLIAN. Never you mind. Here. Do you remember this?

She holds up GLORIA's old ukulele.

Beat.

GLORIA. No.

JILLIAN. Come off it, Glor. Of course you do!

GLORIA. Put that back.

JILLIAN. It's still got your initials on the back. 'GW' Gloria Webb. Look –

GLORIA *(interrupting)*. I SAID PUT IT BACK.

And stop acting the goat. I'm not in the mood.

Beat.

RUBY (*reading*). 'May third. Mr and Mrs Arthur Tattersall, Grimsby. "A comfortable stay. PS we could not see the sea."'

Silence.

JILLIAN. Do either of you remember him. Dad? Like. His face?

GLORIA. You seen snaps.

JILLIAN. Aye but –

GLORIA. He looked like that.

JILLIAN. I just wondered. As you know, I wasn't born, Gloria.

GLORIA. Yes you were.

JILLIAN. No I wasn't.

GLORIA. You were.

JILLIAN. All right. What year did Dad's destroyer get torpedoed?

RUBY *and* GLORIA *look at each other. Beat.*

GLORIA. The HMS *Albrighton* was torpedoed by a German U-boat on tenth March, 1943. Dad also died in a POW Camp in Jerez, Spain, September 1944. And at the Battle of El Alamein.

JILLIAN. What are you saying?

GLORIA. What's the name of this house, Jillian?

JILLIAN. Seaview.

GLORIA. I rest my case.

RUBY. I remember a man dressed in white, with a sailor's hat. Coming home, scooping Mum up. Them going off down The Feathers, coming home happy, breath sweet, hiding humbugs down the back of the settee for us to find. Showing us his tattoo. Sliding down banister frontways and breaking his pelvis. Sat in a string vest, in deckchair in the backyard smoking. Mowing the lawn. Selling the lawnmower to the milkman. Arguing with the milkman. Punching the milkman.

Beat.

Mum and him fighting upstairs.

RUBY *puts the guestbook back in the crib. Picks up some sheet music.*

But then again. Who knows? I may have dreamt it. (*Re: the sheet music.*) Here, I remember this one. Do you remember it, Glor?

GLORIA. No.

RUBY. Have a butchers. Here.

She shows her it. GLORIA *doesn't look.*

GLORIA. I said I don't know it. (*To herself.*) Fuckin' sweltering.

RUBY. I used to love this one. Gave me goose pimples.

RUBY *searches for the melody. As she does…*

JILLIAN. Well I was only asking. It's what they do at a moment like this, isn't it. Families. Ask questions. Compare memories. 'I thought the carpet was blue.' 'I think you'll find it was green.' 'What was the goldfish called?' 'What year did Auntie Pam die?'

Beat.

GLORIA. What are you saying, Jillian?

JILLIAN. Nothing.

GLORIA. Good. Auntie Pam. Bloody Goldfish. This is what happens when you spend too much time alone.

JILLIAN. I'm just saying, people remember things differently, don't they? And sometimes people forget things. Things they don't want to remember.

Absentmindedly, JILLIAN *plucks one string of the ukulele. It rings.*

GLORIA *stares forward. Impassive.*

RUBY. Ah… Sod it. It's gone.

She tosses the sheet music aside.

GLORIA. Thank God. You sound like a cat in a mangle.

Enter DENNIS *from upstairs. Buttoning up his shirt.*
JILLIAN *puts the ukelele back in the crib.*

DENNIS. Some like it hot. It's bloody Bali up there.

RUBY. Evening, sexy. Black Magic?

JILLIAN. Where are you?

DENNIS. Massachusetts. It's sodding baking. Where are you?

JILLIAN. Tennessee.

GLORIA. Colorado.

RUBY. Your two are in Alaska. Poor buggers must be dripping off the walls.

DENNIS. How is she?

JILLIAN. Well, you know –

GLORIA. Our mother is in agony, Dennis, thank you very much.

JILLIAN. You off out?

DENNIS. For a walk. It can't be hotter out there, can it?

RUBY. Have fun, love. Try and get back before lunch tomorrow.

DENNIS. I've never been this hot before. I'm confused. I am. I'm very confused.

He walks out.

RUBY. You know if Dennis were to walk out of here and become a missing person, and I had to describe him to the police, I genuinely wouldn't know where to start. What colour would you say those eyes were? The hair? It's almost impossible to say.

Beat.

How would you describe your Bill. To police?

GLORIA. If police come round I'm over the back wall. They'll know it was me what dug the hole.

RUBY *laughs heartily, and starts to choke on a Dreamy Fudge. (NB This should have the feeling that it is the actor, not the character, who is choking.)*

JILLIAN. Christ, Ruby. Breathe.

GLORIA. Breathe, love. Can you breathe.

JILLIAN. Breathe.

GLORIA *gets up to whack* RUBY *on the back…*

GLORIA. Brace yourself! One. Two.

RUBY. I'm back. (*Coughs.*) Christ, I thought I was being gathered there. By a Black Magic.

Pause. (In this pause it should feel like the actors are 'gathering themselves'.)

JILLIAN. Well I think Dennis and Bill are fine men.

RUBY. Ah, Jilly Jilly Lady Baby Singley Jingly Webb! I was always jealous of you. Not stuck here on your little heap of stones, year in year out. No. What I envy is your innocence… I mean look at you! Thirty –

JILLIAN. …Two.

RUBY. Thirty-two and fancy-free! No fat fart clogging up the bog. And no kids! It's genius. Take Barry. Wait. Have you met Barry?

JILLIAN. When he was a baby. And a boy.

RUBY. Well he's fifteen now. And take it from me he's an absolute tit. Marriage is a scam. Babies are prats. Four-year-olds is like living with drunk dwarves. Next minute you turn round, they've got hair on their chest, tossing off into your best bra. Trust me, you've cracked this. Keep it up, love. You're almost home.

JILLIAN. If Dennis is so dull why did you marry him?

RUBY. Do you remember Liam Brown?

JILLIAN. Course I do. He was gorgeous.

RUBY. Liam Brown took my virginity.

GLORIA. Bollocks.

RUBY. Liam Brown took my virginity.

GLORIA. Liam Brown took your virginity.

RUBY. Liam Brown took my virginity. So I started at the very very top. Like. A god. End of that term I asked him to go to the Winter Gardens with me, Liam told me to fuck off. All that summer he were everywhere, that cunt. Ghost Train. Liam's there. So the time came when I said myself, come on, Ruby, sort this out, stop moping over some chopper who works in a chicken factory in Penswick.

GLORIA. Liam Brown was fucking gorgeous.

RUBY. From this day forward, you, Ruby Webb, *you* are Liam Brown. From now on you're choosing blokes that can't believe their fucking luck. 'How did it come to pass that Ruby Webb is mine? I'm walking on air. I'm the luckiest man alive.' Then about a year or two, that lucky man suddenly realises 'Hang about. I'm a sad dull berk.' They get paranoid. Except it's not paranoia. It's true. At this point, they go slowly but surely stark staring mad. Start following you around. Reading your diary. Six months in, they're quivering wrecks. What happens then? Get rid. Find a new one. Trust me. There's tons. Gallons. England may have a water shortage but the one thing She is not short of is dull boring bastards.

JILLIAN. What about Dennis. He's still there.

RUBY. And that, Jillian, is the wonder of Dennis. My Dennis is too dull to go mad. I am entirely safe in the knowledge that he will never, ever leave me, nor break my heart. I'd have left him years ago, but I'm afraid of the dark.

Pause.

GLORIA. So, you never asked her?

JILLIAN. Who?

GLORIA. Who d'you mean who? Mum.

JILLIAN. You could have asked her.

GLORIA. I wasn't here.

JILLIAN. Exactly. It's not an easy topic to raise. 'By the way,
    Mum, I was wondering would you like to be eaten by worms
    or incinerated.'

RUBY. I wouldn't have phrased it like that. It's insensitive.

GLORIA. Easy or not, it might have been wise to raise it before
    she were flat-out, six stone wet through, screaming like
    a bayoneted German.

JILLIAN. I thought when the time came, we could decide
    together, and all chip in.

GLORIA. So us three.

JILLIAN. Aye.

    Beat.

    And Joan.

RUBY. Here we go.

GLORIA. I see. Well when, if, she gets here we can ask her to
    chip in. Who knows? Maybe she'll swan in here and pick up
    the whole bill. In her fucking helicopter. In her sequins, limo,
    a red carpet, a fistful of fuckin'. And lo she doth return. Is
    that Donny and Marie? I don't fucking think so. It's St Joan.
    The Patron Saint of Favourite Children.

JILLIAN. Well if you ask me I think you're being more than
    a little uncharitable. And anyway, mums don't have favourites.

GLORIA (*with venom*). Ha! Who told you that?

    RUBY *is holding the song sheet, trying to find the melody.*

RUBY. You can see her point though.

GLORIA. Who?

RUBY. Mum. Even when Joan were ten she were a star. If we
    had a show, church fete, Brawby, Tabernacle, I'd be stood in

the wings twisting my plaits, knees knocking. Jill'd be there, frock shaking, picking her scabs. You next along. Sweating. With your fucking ukulele. But Joan. Joan would be calm. Still. Like she weren't at the Brawby Fete. Or Tabernacle. Her sequins sparklier. Shoes shinier. And her eyes... It were like they could see clean past the church. Past the fete. Past Blackpool. Like a figurehead. Back straight. Poised. Fresh carved and gilded, on the prow of a galleon bound for distant shores.

Pause.

All these years knowing she's out there, living her life, a free life, with nothing to hold her back or tramp her down. That's what's kept me ticking all these years. It made my life in Rochdale somehow perfectly tolerable. When I lie there at night, with Dennis beside me, I think of her out there. I picture her face. Her smile. Those eyes. In golden sunshine. And I drift off to dreamland.

Pause. She turns to her sisters.

Do you remember what it felt like to sing together?

Enter PENNY, *from upstairs.* JILLIAN *springs up.*

JILLIAN. How is she?

PENNY. I'm afraid your mother is in a great deal of pain.

JILLIAN. Oh no.

PENNY. I'll be here to help. I'm here till the morning. I won't leave you.

JILLIAN. This is my sister Ruby.

RUBY. How do you do?

PENNY. How do you do?

JILLIAN. And this is my sister –

GLORIA. Hello. I'm Gloria. I'm the eldest.

JILLIAN. Joan's the eldest.

Beat.

GLORIA. Firstly, I would like to say thank you for everything you're doing for our mother. Now. Do you mind if I speak plainly? Right now our mother is up there in exquisite torment. She looks like a skull with a rag hanging out of it. Now for pity's sake. Is there not something you can give her?

Beat.

PENNY. Have you not discussed it…?

GLORIA. Discussed what?

JILLIAN. Not as yet. We were going to discuss it.

GLORIA. Discuss what?

Pause.

JILLIAN. So… Peggy…

PENNY (*quietly*). Penny.

Beat.

JILLIAN. So Penny and me, I, Penny and I, earlier, we had a chat… And she, Penny, told… she gave me some information.

Pause.

And basically we were going to discuss it… At an opportune juncture…

Beat.

GLORIA. Discuss what? What were we going to discuss?

JILLIAN. The information.

GLORIA. What information?

Beat.

What information, Jillian?

PENNY. May I?

Beat.

This morning I informed your sister that if you were all in accord, then there were options, unofficial mind you, whereby your mother's needs, such as they are, vis-à-vis suffering and what-have-you... could be addressed.

Silence.

GLORIA. Am I going mad here. What's that in English?

RUBY. A hot shot.

Beat.

Morphine. It puts you to sleep. They gave one to Dennis's dad. I thought it be 'cause he was in the Masons.

Pause.

PENNY. Anyway. She has the number. Should you decide...

JILLIAN *puts her hand in her pocket where the number is.*

GLORIA. Penny. If you don't mind, I'd like to speak to my sister for a moment.

PENNY. I'll be through here.

She goes through to the kitchen. JILLIAN *focuses hard on a photograph album. Turning the pages.*

GLORIA. So I'm just going to check I've got this correct. To be clear, Mum is in purgatory, because we're waiting for someone hasn't set foot in this house for twenty years. Someone who doesn't give half a shit about her and never did.

JILLIAN. I'm busy.

GLORIA. How many times has she phoned? How many letters? Christmas. Birthdays. When the kids were born. When Barry was born, did she call Ruby? Mum wrote to Joan more than a hundred times. Not one reply. That's who we're waiting for. That's why she's in torment. Because of a stranger.

JILLIAN. I made a promise.

GLORIA (*sarcastic*). Well why didn't you say? Have a Black Magic. Where do you want me, skipper? Are you in charge now? Is this your house? The reason you stuck here, chuck, is because you get to corner of street, your knees knock. Up bingo? No fear. Lobster Pot? No fear. 'Well, you could have been here, Gloria.' Cobbler's. Face it. You're not here for Mum. You're hiding. You're here because you can't find the door.

Silence.

JILLIAN. Well. I found it.

RUBY. Found what?

JILLIAN *stands holding a photograph.*

JILLIAN. Mum and Joan, when she was a baby.

She puts it in front of GLORIA.

GLORIA. Aye aye. And what may I ask is that in aid of?

RUBY *sings from the song sheet. She has remembered the melody.*

RUBY (*singing*).
Once I laughed when I heard you saying
That I'd be playing Solitaire –

(*Spoken.*) I've got it.

(*Singing.*) Uneasy in my easy chair
It never entered my mind...

Pause.

(*Spoken, American accent.*) Do you recall that poky little sack joint in Wichita? The Two-Star Quick-Stop Motel. We shared one big bed and lived for a week off a single chicken. One bird, three bottles of Coke and a jar of pickles. And that lasted the week.

Beat.

And then there was that time down in Galveston when we were chased seven blocks by a whole swarm of sailors.

Pause.

JILLIAN (*American*). Those boys chased us like hyenas. Heck, LaVerne, we only just got away with our virtue intact.

RUBY. No kidding, Maxene. That was a long, lonely night for the US Navy.

JILLIAN *and* RUBY. And no mistake!

Beat.

RUBY (*singing*).
And once you told me I was mistaken
That I'd awaken with the sun
And order orange juice for one
It never entered my mind

Softly, JILLIAN *joins in.*

RUBY *and* JILLIAN (*singing*).
You had what I lack, myself
Now I even have to scratch my back myself

JILLIAN (*singing*).
Once you warned me that if you scorned me
I'd say the maiden's prayer again

RUBY *and* JILLIAN (*singing*).
And wish that you were there again
To get into my hair again
It never entered my mind

Pause.

JILLIAN. Why do you think Joan never came back?

Suddenly:

VERONICA. Joan!

YOUNG JOAN. Coming, Mum!

Enter YOUNG JOAN.

(*NB None of the sisters see her, nor she them.*)

YOUNG JOAN *puts a coin in the Lucky Lady. Pulls the handle.*

Come on come on come on!

Jackpot. It spills out coins.

Yes!

VERONICA (*from upstairs*). Jo-an!

YOUNG JOAN. Coming, Mum!

She scoops up the coins. And hurries through to –

The kitchen –

The next moment we are back in 1955.

Someone has done everything they possibly can to create an atmosphere. A checkered red-and-white tablecloth. Candles in wine bottles.

YOUNG JOAN *puts on a cardigan, and hurries outside.*

Enter VERONICA.

In make-up, red lipstick, pencil skirt, fishnets, holding three or four silk scarves…

Looking at her watch. She drapes the scarves over lamps.

She knocks a vase of flowers over. It smashes.

VERONICA. Shitehawks…

She flies into action, picking up the pieces with a dustpan and brush.

JOE *appears from the street.*

Jog Fogg, where've you been?

JOE. I'm sorry, Mrs Webb. The tram died.

VERONICA. It's ten to!

JOE. I had to run all the way from Star Gate. I'll have a quick swim round the bath.

VERONICA. There's no time. Give yourself a wash with flannel, get straight down. (*Calling.*) Gloria!

YOUNG GLORIA (*from upstairs*). Nearly ready, Mum!

Enter YOUNG RUBY *and* YOUNG JILLIAN.

YOUNG JILLIAN. Mum! What's wrong? We heard a smash.

VERONICA. Why aren't you ready? Come on. Get from under the feet! Up! Up!

YOUNG RUBY. Mum, I'm shaking. I've got a stomachful of squirrels.

YOUNG JILLIAN. *I'm* the one's shaking. I'm going to wet me knickers!

YOUNG RUBY. Gloria's up there sweating like a pig.

VERONICA. Listen to me. Both of you. Ruby, you are not shaking. Jillian, you are not going to wet your knickers. And Gloria is not up there sweating like a pig. Is that clear?

YOUNG RUBY. Yes, Mum.

YOUNG JILLIAN. Yes, Mum.

VERONICA. Good. Now go on... Get!

They run out.

JOE. It looks lovely in here. Very chic.

VERONICA. Well I don't know about that. There was this photo of a French café in *Woman's Own*. But this looks nothing like it.

JOE. And you too. You look lovely.

VERONICA. Give over.

JOE. I mean it. Your lasses are lucky to have such a mother!

VERONICA *is suddenly taken aback. She hugs* JOE, *tightly.*

VERONICA. Joe, what we've made, we've made together. And whatever's coming, well... we're not leaving anyone behind here. You understand?

JOE. This night. This room. It's like a dream already.

BIDDY *comes in from the public parlour.*

BIDDY. Mrs Webb. (*Stops.*) Excuse me. Am I interrupting?

They break.

VERONICA (*to* JOE). Come on. Stir tha' stumps… Biddy. Have you washed the windows?

BIDDY. Yes, Mrs Webb.

VERONICA. Mousetraps?

BIDDY. Out of sight, Mrs Webb.

VERONICA. Good. Public parlour please. No one plays the Lucky Lady and no one, and I mean no one is to come through. Is that clear?

BIDDY. Don't worry, Mrs Webb. I'll guard that door with my life.

BIDDY *exits.*

Suddenly –

YOUNG JOAN (*offstage*). MUM!

Enter YOUNG JOAN, *from outside.*

VERONICA. Joan. What are you doing? You're not in your costume…

YOUNG JOAN. Mum. They're here.

Beat.

VERONICA (*to herself*). They're here… (*Shouting.*) THEY'RE H–

She bolts back across the kitchen to the foot of the stairs.

Girls. They're here! (*To* YOUNG JOAN.) Right. Upstairs. I'll keep them talking. Three minutes. You hear. Three!

YOUNG JOAN. Yes, Mum!

They hug quickly. She runs upstairs. YOUNG GLORIA *appears halfway.*

YOUNG GLORIA. I can't find my ukelele! It's gone!

YOUNG JOAN. It's under your bed.

YOUNG GLORIA. Joan.

YOUNG JOAN stops.

I'm scared.

YOUNG JOAN. No you're not. You're Gloria. And what's Gloria?

YOUNG GLORIA. Hip.

YOUNG JOAN. Hip as what?

YOUNG GLORIA. Hip as fuck.

They hug, and scurry upstairs.

In the kitchen, VERONICA *pours herself a drink, and leans on the piano.*

Under her breath, she practises a very quick greeting. Expressions. She is incredibly tense. Shaking.

VERONICA. Oh God.

She drinks the drink. Closes her eyes, takes a breath.

Enter JACK, *followed by* LUTHER ST JOHN, *an American, forties. In a suit.*

JACK. Come through, Luther. Now there's lovely. (*Stops. Joking.*) Eh up. No one's home. Let's back down pub!

He turns around.

VERONICA. No you don't, Jack Larkin.

VERONICA *approaches, super-relaxed.*

JACK (*American 'movie' accent*). And then in the shadows, something was moving. A vampire? (*Normal voice.*) Well you ask me, that is a pretty tasty vampire. Veronica. You didn't have to make all this effort just for me? I'm joking.

VERONICA. Give over, Jack.

JACK. Veronica, this is Mr Luther St John. Luther, this is
Veronica Webb.

LUTHER. Pleasure to meet you, Mrs Webb.

VERONICA. Now I absolutely insist you call me Veronica.

JACK. Not 'Ronnie'. You'll get a slap on the bum for that. And
trust me, it stings.

Beat.

VERONICA. Do me a favour, Jack. Pop up and give Joe a shout.

JACK. Ah, he'll be down.

VERONICA. And then pop back down...

JACK *twigs.*

JACK (*posh*). Aye, my queen. I shall venture forth. And upon my
triumphant return... (*Northern.*) mine's a Scotch and soda.

*He pinches her behind and heads out. She absolutely does
not react.*

VERONICA. So, Mr St John.

LUTHER. Call me Luther.

VERONICA. So I've never met an American before, so forgive
me, I don't know what they eat or drink. I've got Campari,
gin or Scotch. Best I could afford which is cheap as chips.

LUTHER. Scotch.

VERONICA (*to herself*). Well there's lovely. (*Hums.*) So,
Luther, my first question is why on God's earth is Perry
Como's agent friends with a berk like Jack Larkin.

LUTHER *smiles.*

LUTHER. So you're a widow.

VERONICA. Aye. My husband, Mr Webb, was killed in action.
D-Day, sixth of June, 1944. He was on the beach there,
saving the life of an American soldier. A corporal he was...
from Brooklyn.

From the way she says it, this is clearly inside information.

LUTHER. Well it's a small world. I'm from Greenpoint.

VERONICA. Isn't that a coincidence. I'm not gonna lie, it's been hard yards, and there's been times when I've wanted to cry, or throttle one of them, but what good does crying ever do, at the end of the day?

LUTHER *smiles. (During the following the* GIRLS *creep down the stairs to assemble in the public parlour, out of view.)*

LUTHER. This is a kitchen.

VERONICA. No flies on you! Through there's the public parlour. And in order to rehearse without the great unwashed of Lancashire breathing down our necks, we've had to make do.

She hands him his drink. He drinks half of it.

Means I can keep an eye on things. Although the acoustics in here is dire. So please disregard that. Anyroad, I'm sure you'll spot it.

LUTHER. Few years back I was down in Alabama in the cold-water shack of a then-undiscovered coloured artist. The piano was in the bathtub, the bass fiddle was poking out the chimney.

VERONICA. Give over!

LUTHER. That was the home of Nathaniel Adams Coles.

Pause. She tries not to sound staggered as she says.

VERONICA. Nat King Cole.

LUTHER. I'm no snob, Mrs Webb. I like down and dirty.

LUTHER *lights a cigarette.* VERONICA *stands watching him exhale smoke.*

As VERONICA *fetches a saucer as an ashtray,* JACK *reappears with* JOE. *He registers the smoke. So does* JOE.

JACK. Aye aye… What's this? Six-thirty and talking dirty! She's letting it all hang out tonight, Luther! Yes, sir! Anything goes!

VERONICA. Luther. This is Joe Fogg. My pianist.

LUTHER. Pleasure to meet you, Joe.

JOE (*very nervous*). Fogg. Joe Fogg. I'm a big fan of Perry.
    I can't believe I'm saying that. Perry. Like I know him.
    I don't know him. How would I possibly.

LUTHER. I'll let Mr Como know.

VERONICA. Joe, let me fettle your tie there.

As she straightens JOE*'s tie, she asks quietly:*

Ready?

JOE (*quietly*). They're ready.

LUTHER. So. Should we do this?

VERONICA. Absolutely. Joseph. Positions *s'il vous plaît.*

As they prepare, JACK *refills his glass with Scotch.*

JACK. Luther old son, this time next year you're going to get
    down on your knees and thank me. (*American accent.*) Yes
    siree, these chicks are smokin', daddio!

LUTHER. Do me a favour, Jack.

He gestures for JACK *to move back.*

VERONICA. Now remember, the eldest is fifteen, so go easy,
    they're not the finished article. Also, as I say, the acoustics –

JACK (*calling*). Enough sizzle. Let's see the sausage!

Beat.

VERONICA. So. Ladies and gentlemen…

Pause.

Ladies and gentlemen. The Seaview Luxury Guest House
and Spa presents: the Webb Sisters!

JOE *hits a rolling barrel-house groove.*

Suddenly –

The GIRLS *burst from behind the curtain in a tap-dancing conga line.* YOUNG GLORIA *with her ukulele. They are wearing matching stars-and-stripes outfits.*

They gather in front of the piano and go into a tight routine.

GIRLS (*singing*).
He was a famous trumpet man from out Chicago way
He had a boogie style that no one else could play
He was the top man at his craft
But then his number came up and he was gone with the draft
He's in the army now, a-blowin' reveille
He's the boogie woogie bugle boy of Company B!

They made him blow a bugle for his Uncle Sam
It really brought him down because he couldn't jam
The captain seemed to understand
Because the next day the cap went out and drafted a band
And now the company jumps when he plays reveille
He's the boogie woogie bugle boy of Company B!

A toot, a toot, a toot diddleyada toot
He blows it eight to the bar in boogie rhythm
He can't blow a note unless the bass and guitar is playin'
    with him
He makes the company jump when he plays reveille
He's the boogie woogie bugle boy of Company B!
Yes sir!

YOUNG JOAN (*singing*).
He was a boogie woogie bugle boy of Company B
And when he plays boogie woogie bugle he was busy as a
    buzz bee
And when he plays he makes the company jump eight to the
    bar
He's the boogie woogie bugle boy of Company B!

Toot toot toot toot diddleyada toot toot
He blows it eight to the bar
He can't blow a note if the bass and guitar isn't with him
A-a-a-and the company jumps when he plays reveille
He's the boogie woogie bugle boy of Company B!

Tap break.

GIRLS (*singing*).
 Da dah da dah da da da
 Da dah da dah da da da
 Dah dah dah da da da da
 Da dah da dah da da da
 A-a-a-and the company jumps when he plays reveille
 He's the boogie woogie bugle boy of Company B!

They hoof, tap-dance and play their hearts out. Throughout
VERONICA *keeps time, and half an eye on* LUTHER.

At the middle eight, VERONICA *realizes* YOUNG GLORIA
doesn't have her ukulele. She tries to make getting it to her
part of the routine, as if it was always planned.

The GIRLS *climax by tap-dancing on the table, into a beam-*
ing tableau.

JACK (*clapping, nudging* LUTHER). See, St John. What did
 I tell ya?! That's why they call me Jackpot!

They go straight into 'Straighten Up and Fly Right'.

JOE. Three four.

GIRLS (*singing*).
 A buzzard took a monkey for a ride in the air
 The monkey thought that everything was on the square –

LUTHER *holds up his hands…*

LUTHER. Thank you. Thank you.

They come to a stop. Pause.

 What are your names…?

VERONICA. Go on. He won't bite!

YOUNG RUBY. Ruby.

YOUNG JILLIAN. I'm Jillian. Jill for short.

YOUNG GLORIA. I'm Gloria.

YOUNG JOAN. I'm Joan.

LUTHER. Well, girls, you did a swell job.

VERONICA. Say thank you… / Honestly.

ALL. Thank you. / Thank you.

Pause.

LUTHER. Veronica. I'd like to speak to you alone if I may.

Beat.

VERONICA. Right. Public parlour please, girls.

JACK. Remember who tipped you the wink. Old Jack Larkin knows his onions.

He corrals the GIRLS *through to the parlour.*

Here, girls. I bought a stepladder but I'm worried about introducing it to my real ladder!

As they go, YOUNG JOAN *hugs* YOUNG GLORIA, *reassuringly.*

Everybody heads through to the parlour.

In the kitchen, VERONICA *and* LUTHER *are alone.*

LUTHER. It's The Andrews Sisters.

Beat.

VERONICA. Full marks. But as you no doubt know The Andrews Sisters were heavily influenced in their time by The Boswell Sisters. Who in turn were influenced by –

LUTHER. What is it you want?

Pause.

VERONICA. Golly. Well.

Pause.

I'm going to be honest with you now. Luther, I've heard these girls do 'Boogie Woogie Bugle Boy' a thousand times and I swear to God I still get goose pimples. I think the sky's the limit. So yes, I'd like one or possibly more of the theatres here in Blackpool, so that they can get used to playing bigger rooms. For example. The London Palladium. You asked. I'm just being honest. And it's not pie in the sky. Mae Ray went from The Alhambra to the Palladium to Carnegie Hall in six months. Also, teaming with a star, your Tommy Steeles, your Bobby Darins, and, if I may be so bold, your Perry Comos… The Andrews did it with Bing and Dean et cetera. It made a smash package.

LUTHER. And now Miss Ray makes a thousand dollars a night.

VERONICA. Well all I can say is jeepers creepers. That would pay for a lot of laundry.

LUTHER. Nat King Cole makes twenty thousand. I took a big bite of that. It's one of the reasons he fired me.

Beat.

VERONICA. My God. You can… you can see it, can't you? You can see what I see. Can you?

LUTHER. Next month there's a gala evening I'm helping put together. A charity event, with a whole roster. Some household names. Some new faces. It's at the London Palladium.

VERONICA. Oh God.

LUTHER *nods.*

LUTHER. But see, I'm afraid there's a problem.

Beat.

VERONICA. So. Can I stop you there because I think I know where this is going. No please because I've thought this through very, very carefully. They're four girls, and the Andrews and the Boswells are three. Three seats in the boat. But, that's not a disadvantage. Because as I see it, we've got one spare. In the wings. LaVerne Andrews was forever falling sick. Tickly coughs, laryngitis. The show's shot. Not ours. We've got a spare wheel. Waiting. But in the background. And I think it's clear from watching them, even in here, that that person is Gloria.

YOUNG GLORIA *steps forward on the stairs. She has been listening.*

LUTHER. If you don't mind me saying, that's a tough call for
a mother to make.

VERONICA. It's common sense. Business. And who knows
that better than you?

Pause.

LUTHER. So that's not the problem.

Pause.

This style. This type of music. It's not what the public want
today.

Silence.

VERONICA. This is popular music.

LUTHER. It *was*.

Pause.

VERONICA. I think you'll find it *is*.

Pause.

I think. Okay. This is an opportunity, sir. What we, they, my
girls, have, is rare. The theatres, they need it. The audiences
want it. You can't tell me this isn't the ticket.

LUTHER. It *was* the ticket.

VERONICA. No. No. Forgive me, but you're wrong. Not wrong.
Mistaken… I'm sorry but I won't have it. No *no*. I won't.
I won't stand here have you tell me that my girls. All right.

Pause.

So yes, Patty decided to break away to be a soloist. She had
married the pianist, Walter Weschler, who as I'm sure you
know became The Andrews Sisters' manager and that drove
a wedge between them. And they found out from the gossip
columns. That was naughty of her. And 'The Windmill Song'
was not strong material. Then Maxene tried to commit
suicide. But the audience, the audience is there! Millions of
them. And the sisters splitting up only means there's

a massive gap. Ruby, Jill and Joan, with Gloria, are going to show the world who they are. I know it. I know it like it's already happened. Because it has. You know where. Here.

She opens her arms.

You said this is the type of place, this kitchen… Down and dirty. Plus… Like you say… There's money to be made. So my question is. Are you the man who's going to benefit from that. Let me ask you another question. Let me… Hang on. Here's an important question. Here's an important question. What is a song?

LUTHER. Have you heard of Elvis Presley?

Silence.

VERONICA. I'm sorry. I don't know what that is.

Pause.

LUTHER. Presley. Elvis Presley.

Pause.

VERONICA. I don't know what that is.

Pause.

I don't understand… Why are you telling me about a gala in London. Why. The sodding. The Palladium, then… I don't understand.

Pause.

LUTHER. Sit down, Veronica…

VERONICA. I don't understand.

She does.

LUTHER. When I walked into that shack in Montgomery, and I heard that young coloured boy sing, I knew as plain as day I was looking at a star.

Pause.

You can't fake it. It's there, like the rain. Like fire.

Pause.

I don't see that here. Except in one of your girls.

Pause.

VERONICA. All right. Fine. Which one?

LUTHER. Joan.

Pause.

VERONICA. Well, Mr… Well, Luther… I'm not surprised.
Because Joan. Joan is indeed very talented. However –

LUTHER. Nathaniel Adams was in a trio when I met him.
Seventeen years old. Nat King Cole is the biggest-selling
artist in the history of Capitol Records.

Pause.

With your permission, I'd like to speak with her.

Beat.

VERONICA. Now?

Pause.

LUTHER. It's up to you.

Silence. VERONICA *sits there. She looks as if she's about to
launch into a whole new defence.*

Instead, she goes to the door of the parlour. As she does,
YOUNG GLORIA *hides.*

VERONICA. Joan. Will you come through here please?

YOUNG JOAN *appears.*

Joan? Will you come through here please.

YOUNG JOAN *walks in.*

LUTHER. Hello, Joan.

YOUNG JOAN. Hello.

VERONICA. Mr St John would like to speak to you, Joan.

Pause.

LUTHER. That was quite a performance.

YOUNG JOAN. Thank you.

LUTHER. Do you enjoy this? Or is Mom putting you up to it. Would you rather be out with the other kids, playing?

YOUNG JOAN. No. I love singing and dancing.

LUTHER. So. Who do you like?

YOUNG JOAN *looks at her mother.*

YOUNG JOAN. I like The Andrews Sisters.

LUTHER. Who else?

YOUNG JOAN. Johnny Mercer. Johnny Hartman. Fats Domino. Fats Waller. Nat King Cole.

LUTHER. You like Nat?

YOUNG JOAN. I love him.

Beat.

Nat King Cole is hip.

LUTHER *smiles.* VERONICA *looks confused. Pause.*

LUTHER. Joan, how would it be if you were to sing for me without your sisters?

YOUNG JOAN *looks at her mother, who gives a small nod.*

YOUNG JOAN. That would be all right. I suppose.

LUTHER. Would you like that?

YOUNG JOAN. I suppose so.

LUTHER. What would you like to sing? I know. How about some Nat King Cole. You said you're a fan?

Pause.

YOUNG JOAN. Do you know 'When I Fall in Love'?

LUTHER. Are you kidding me? I bought that tune. I bought that song for Nat. Would you like to sing it?

VERONICA. Hang about, Joan. I. No. I don't think that's right. Sing 'Dream a Little Dream of Me'? Or 'Along the Navajo Trail'.

YOUNG JOAN. But, Mum –

VERONICA. 'Tuxedo Junction'. Sing 'Dream a Little Dream of Me'. 'Dream a Little Dream of' –

LUTHER. Why don't you let her sing what she wants to sing?

Beat.

YOUNG JOAN. I'd like to sing 'When I Fall in Love'. Is that all right, Mum?

Beat.

LUTHER. Is that all right, Veronica?

Beat.

VERONICA. I think 'When I Fall in Love' is an excellent choice.

LUTHER. Well okay. Sing it for me now. Just you. Right here. Just your voice.

Pause.

YOUNG JOAN. Mum?

VERONICA. It's okay, Joan. It's okay.

YOUNG JOAN smiles at her mother.

Silence. She draws breath to sing…

YOUNG JOAN (*singing*).
When I fall in love
It will be forever –

LUTHER (*interrupting*). Nope. No. No. No. This isn't gonna work.

Beat.

Veronica, I was wrong, you were right. The acoustics in here are shot. Is there anywhere else we could go?

VERONICA. What?

LUTHER. Is there another room? This room is horrible. It's killing my ears.

VERONICA. There isn't another room. There's the public parlour but –

LUTHER. Well then I guess that's too bad. Oh well. All the same, thanks, Joan. And good luck with everything. You got a swell voice. I really hope –

YOUNG JOAN. Mississippi.

Beat.

LUTHER. Excuse me?

YOUNG JOAN. Mississippi.

Beat.

VERONICA. It's silly actually. The rooms have all got names. Colorado. Alabama. Indiana. Minnesota. It's just a bit of fun. But –

LUTHER. Where's Mississippi?

YOUNG JOAN. It's upstairs.

LUTHER. Will you show me?

VERONICA. Joan –

YOUNG JOAN. It's all right, Mum. (*To* LUTHER.) I'll show you.

Beat.

VERONICA. Mr St John.

LUTHER. Is there a problem, Veronica?

Beat.

VERONICA. I was just thinking. Perhaps you and I could go up to Mississippi and discuss this.

Pause.

LUTHER. Why?

Pause.

VERONICA. I was just saying. There's lots to discuss. And we could go to Mississippi and discuss it. You and me.

LUTHER. Forgive me, but you're not the talent here.

Pause.

Now I would like to hear your daughter sing. Alone. If that's a problem –

VERONICA. It's not a problem.

LUTHER. Then what's the problem?

Beat.

Look it was swell to meet you both. I wish you all the best. Veronica, please tell Jack I had to go. Good evening, ladies.

He turns and heads out.

VERONICA. Joan.

He stops. Pause.

Show Luther Mississippi.

Pause.

LUTHER. Joan?

Beat.

YOUNG JOAN. It's this way. Follow me.

LUTHER. After you.

They head upstairs.

VERONICA *stands alone.*

JOE *comes out of the parlour, and enters the kitchen.*

JOE. Mrs Webb.

VERONICA. Not now, Joe.

JOE. Where have they gone?

VERONICA. You hold your whisht, now, Joe. Everything's under control.

JOE. Where's Joan? Mrs Webb?

Pause.

Mrs Webb. Where's Joan? What's happening?

Pause.

VERONICA. What's happening? I'll tell you what's happening. This was it. Tonight. Everything I've worked for. And what happens? You show up, late, reeking of booze, with some cock-and-bull about the tram. I give you a hug and it's like I'm hugging a pub. I told you over and over. Did you listen? And now everyone knows best. Everyone knows what's best for my girls. Well as it happens. Luther has made me an offer. That's right. No thanks to you. And not Blackpool. The London Palladium. There's a gala night he's organising and. (*Stops.*) And he asked me what *I* wanted. 'What do you want, Veronica?' His words. And I told him. Do you know how much Nat King Cole gets per show? Twenty thousand dollars. Per show. So don't come in here telling me what's what. Like you know the score because you don't, Joe Fogg. Because I know what's right. I know what's right for my girls. Not you. Not anyone. Me.

She goes to the piano, opens it, takes out a bottle and hands it to him, with his hat.

First thing in the morning I want you out of here. I mean it. Sling your hook. You can keep this month's rent, I don't need it. You know who does? You. Because you're out. You're no' but a pain in my backside. Now get out of my sight. Go on. Get out! And don't you ever, *ever* come back.

Silence.

JOE. I'll be back in the morning to clear out.

He goes to the door. Stops.

God have mercy on you.

He leaves. VERONICA *stands. Very distantly, we hear* YOUNG JOAN…

YOUNG JOAN (*singing*).
    When I fall in love
    It will be forever
    Or I'll never fall in love
    In a restless world like this is
    Love is ended before it's begun…

VERONICA *suddenly finds hope. She sobs.*

And too many moonlight kisses
Seem to cool in the warmth of the sun

When I give my heart, it –

The singing suddenly stops. Silence. In the kitchen, VERONICA *stands motionless.*

On the stairs, YOUNG GLORIA *stands motionless.*

VERONICA *stares ahead. Silence.*

Black.

End of Act Two.

ACT THREE

The public parlour.

A distant church bell strikes three.

BILL *has a toolbox out, and is trying to fix the jukebox. The back is off. The guts are out.*

Enter DENNIS (*from where he enters he doesn't see* BILL).

DENNIS *pours himself the dregs of the gin. Tops it up with the dregs of the Baileys. He sits.*

DENNIS (*to himself*). To Veronica.

> *Drinks.*

BILL. Evening, Dennis.

> DENNIS *jumps out of his skin. Coughs and splutters. Choking…*

DENNIS. Jesus!

BILL. Dennis…

DENNIS. Suffering shit!

BILL. Goodness gracious.

DENNIS. Screaming blue baby Jesus on the cross! What you playing at, man…?!

BILL. Goodness.

DENNIS. Holy moly.

BILL. Breathe, Dennis.

DENNIS. You bastard.

BILL. Breathe, pal.

DENNIS. Holy cock.

BILL. That's it…

DENNIS. Christ.

BILL. Here. / Drink this.

DENNIS. My fucking chips, Bill.

BILL. How's / that?

DENNIS. Jesus.

BILL. You all right now, Dennis.

Beat.

DENNIS. I'm fine.

BILL. You sure, pal? Take your time. In out. There. How's that. There. Now there's lovely. You're right as rain. Hand on heart. I cannot apologise –

DENNIS. Jesus.

BILL. I cannot apologise enough.

Pause.

You're back late.

DENNIS. What?

BILL. I'm just saying. Or early, depending on –

DENNIS. Aye.

BILL. Been anywhere nice? On your excursions.

DENNIS. Y'what?

BILL. Your manoeuvres.

DENNIS. I were just walking about, Bill.

Beat.

So where are we?

BILL. Right. Basically, we're on tenterhooks.

DENNIS. Right.

BILL. We're clinging on.

DENNIS. She's a strong bird.

BILL. She was always strong, aye. Strong, welcoming. A lovely woman. A fine, decent, honest person who's lived a difficult life. But try fitting that on a gravestone. Ignore me. It's the heat.

DENNIS. Telling me. That porch. You could bake scones in there.

BILL. Colorado's a furnace. And when you factor in the snoring.

DENNIS. Snoring?

BILL. Gloria.

DENNIS. Gloria's a snorer?

BILL. Like King Kong, full of sherry. Soon as I was dispatched to the Co-op I thought, 'Here we go, Bill. You, sire, are going to lie there in a hundred and twenty degrees, for six hours, listening to Godzilla get devoured.'

DENNIS *is gazing at the jukebox, vacantly.*

DENNIS. Well I'll say this. That is a lot of wires.

BILL. You what? Oh. Spaghetti Junction, pal.

DENNIS. Do you know what you're doing?

BILL. Me? Nary a clue. I'm having a fiddle. Poke about.

DENNIS. Well it's a shame. There's some foot-tappers.

(*Singing.*) Good Golly Miss Molly, sure like to ball

BILL. An euphemism, Dennis. Yankee slang for sexual congress. A bit of the other.

DENNIS. Summer 1962. Tower Ballroom. I took Ruby to see Little Richard. Our second date. Supported by a little-known band from Liverpool.

BILL. Give over.

DENNIS. No one had a clue. Ruby and me – we were there for Richard. When his band struck up. The drums. Like Hannibal's elephants. After we watched Richard and his

band pile back on his bus, quiff gleaming, teeth shining, and
drive off into the night. Suddenly Ruby dashed forward, out
of the crowd, and cried 'Take me with you! Please.
Wherever you are going. Take me!' But the bus drove away,
and she turned back, and came back over to me. And we
went and got chips.

BILL. If you ask me it went 'Rock Around the Clock', up, up,
up, up. 'Eleanor Rigby'. Down.

DENNIS. Drugs.

BILL. And then suddenly, without anyone consulting you. It
went potty.

DENNIS. Lipstick. Sequins. Sparkly boots.

BILL. Enough's enough. Elkie Brooks. David Bowie. 'Look at
you up there with your hand on your hip. Are you the other
way?' Although, and don't get me wrong, Bryan Ferry is
a very handsome man.

Silence.

DENNIS. Do you miss it?

BILL. Miss what?

DENNIS. Being young.

Silence.

BILL. Here. I forgot to say. Earlier, down here. Huge ding-dong.

DENNIS. Whoops.

BILL. Jill and Gloria. Major square-up. Hammer and tongs.
End of tethers. And lo, the floorboards did shake. I saw your
Ruby duck into Massachusetts. She was in floods. You might
want to pop up there.

DENNIS. What was it about?

BILL. Three guesses. Gloria tends not to talk about her much,
but when she's had a few gins, usually around gin five or six,
the name suddenly pops up. The stories come out. Or,
I should say, the story.

DENNIS. What story?

BILL. You must have heard the story. You know they had this quartet.

DENNIS. Aye. The quartet.

BILL. The quartet. But Joan? Joan wanted to be the star. The prima donna. Her mum said 'Hey you, get in line, and leave the boys alone, sew your knickers to your vest. Or you, young madam, will come to a sticky end.' And lo, it did come to pass.

DENNIS. What happened.

BILL. What usually happens. Young Joan got herself in trouble. Fifteen years old.

DENNIS. Whoops-a-daisy.

BILL *mimes nine months of gestation.*

BILL. It was the beginning of the end for the Seaview Hotel. Abortion. Boat to America. Never been back. So long. Toodle-oo. Hide nor hair.

DENNIS. So hang about. She went to America.

BILL. So here's the facts because I've heard them a hundred times. She went to the U-S of A, cut a record. Last we heard she was living in a commune in Frisco. On the wacky baccy no doubt. Or worse still, chasing the dragon. (*Funny voice.*) Street parlance for injecting the demon poppy – (*Normal voice.*) aka heroin.

DENNIS. I did not know that.

BILL. You just have to put two and two together, Dennis. I mean, where is she? Her mother, her what gave her life, is up there drawing her final breaths, and where is she? Gloria's called the doctor. He'll be here at the crack of dawn. Where's Joan?

Feet on the stairs. Enter TONY.

DENNIS. All right, Tony. What are you doing up?

TONY. What was all that row about? Earlier?

Beat.

BILL. Oh that. It were nowt.

TONY. Aunt Ruby were crying. I could hear her through the wall.

Pause.

DENNIS. Well you know what? I fancy a wander.

BILL. You're not gonna pop up?

Beat.

DENNIS. Aye. Aye, I will. I'll just you know… Give her a minute… Get some fresh air. Touch wood there's a breeze. Night, Bill. Night, Tony.

Beat.

BILL. Night, Dennis.

TONY. Night night, Uncle Dennis.

DENNIS (*quietly singing*).
Tutti frutti, oh rootie
A wop bop a loo bop a lop bam boom

Exit DENNIS.

Beat.

TONY. Dad.

BILL. Aye?

TONY. Why does Mum hate Aunt Joan?

Pause.

BILL. All I know, whatever happened, it were a long time ago.

Pause.

But will you promise me something? You and Patricia… Be kind to each other.

Beat.

Will you do that for me?

TONY. I'll try.

BILL. Good lad.

Pause.

Night, Tony.

TONY. Night, Dad.

TONY *starts to leave. Stops in the doorway. Then he comes over and gives his father a kiss.*

TONY *leaves.* BILL *is alone. He thinks for a moment. Moves over to the jukebox. Plugs it in.*

BILL. Well… Here goes nothing.

He switches it on. Nothing.

BILL *goes upstairs.*

Silence.

Suddenly the jukebox lights come on. It puts on a record. 'Gimme Shelter' by The Rolling Stones. The song plays to the empty parlour.

Enter JOAN.

'Gimme Shelter' plays. JOAN *looks around the room. Not much has changed.*

She moves into the kitchen.

She goes over to the piano. Opens it. Looks at it.

JILLIAN *comes down the stairs. Goes into the parlour to turn off the jukebox. The music stops.*

JILLIAN *comes into the kitchen.* JOAN *is standing at the piano.*

JOAN (*American accent*). Was the piano always here? I'd a laid a hundred it was over there.

JILLIAN. My God. Joan!

JILLIAN *rushes over and hugs her.*

Oh my goodness. My goodness. Sit down. Are you hungry. Let me look at you. My God. It's you! It's really you. You came. I knew you would. Sit down, sit down. Would you like a cup of tea. There was some gin.

JOAN. Thanks. I brought my own.

She takes out a flask. Offers it.

Want some? It's Wild Turkey.

JILLIAN. Gosh. I don't think I've. (*Stops.*) Blow it. I don't mind if I do. Hang about.

She fetches glasses.

I just won a pound. I bet Ruby and Gloria fifty pee each that you'd make it and here you are.

Beat.

JOAN. So they're here.

JILLIAN. Aye. Now Gloria has brung her little ones. Who are not so little. Patty and Anthony. He prefers Tony. Bit naughty. It was strictly no children – but Bill's sister, Joyce – Joyce let them down. Then they had a shocker with the M1 Motorway. What with the heat. But Dennis and Ruby found the M6 not too bad, plus they have air-conditioning. Ruby and Dennis are in Massachusetts. Bill and Gloria – Colorado. I'm in Tennessee, where I've basically been since you last saw me. There's a nurse, Alice, but she's in Scarborough. Her anniversary. So now there's Peggy. Penny. Penny has six boys. I think that's everything.

Beat.

But basically, it's not good. Basically, we're at the crossroads… Barring miracles. Basically, how long's –

She controls tears. Then manages, softly:

…a piece of string?

She gathers herself.

Look at me. Boring you with the – (*Stops.*) I cannot tell you, Joan. I just… (*Brightly.*) And now… Now I've won a pound!

JOAN *nods. Pause.*

JOAN. Have you elected a scapegoat?

Beat.

JILLIAN. Sorry?

JOAN. First thing in a crisis. Ancient times, soon as some major shit went down – war, famine, death of the pharaoh – first thing you do, find a goat. Put all your shit on its head – fear, shame, iniquity, whatever you got – and you let it loose, out into the wilderness. Then you hunt it down, cut out its heart and burn it as an offering to the gods. Have you done that yet? Did I miss it?

Beat.

Well, I guess the night is young.

Beat.

JILLIAN. Now, I must warn you she looks very unwell. I'm not going to lie. It's a shock. And her mind is… But she has moments, moments of whatnot. Clarity. But I absolutely guarantee, one hundred percent she will know it's you.

JOAN. Shit.

Pats herself down.

JILLIAN. What?

JOAN. I'm out of smokes.

JILLIAN. I've got some.

JOAN. You smoke?

JILLIAN. Here.

She gives her a cigarette.

JOAN. What the fuck, Jill. I turn my back… Do you do blow? Drop acid?

She lights it for her.

Thanks.

JILLAN *sits and lights hers. They smoke.*

I see Gowers is gone.

JILLIAN. Aye. It has.

Beat.

JOAN. Old Mr Gower used to give me cigarettes. At the end of the day, when Mrs Gower had gone somewhere, Mr. Gower would close the store, we'd go in the backyard, and I'd sing 'Nature Boy'. And Mr Gower'd sit there with his apron on, in a deck chair with his eyes closed. By the end he'd had tears rolling down his cheeks. Then he'd break open a pack of Player's No.6. And give me three cigarettes. I didn't know it then, but that was probably the most satisfying professional relationship of my entire career.

They smoke.

Pause.

JILLIAN. Joan, I'm a virgin.

JOAN. I'm sorry to hear that.

JILLIAN. What I mean is. Life hasn't. (*Stops.*) Okay. Let me –

She takes a deep breath.

A few weeks back Mother called to me, I went in, and she said something. She said, 'I am not a mother. I am a thing with no soul. I deserve no pity. No pardon. For I am a monster. And death is my only hope.'

Beat.

And then she told me.

Pause.

Joan, I. I had no idea. I, how awful it must have been. For you. For you and yes, for Mum. All these years. I –

JOAN *stands.*

JOAN (*interrupting*). Seriously? You've been here the whole time? That's some sacrifice. But then, I guess we all have our thing. Our skill. Our… talent. I guess that was Mom's.

JILLIAN. What?

Beat.

JOAN. Sacrifice.

They hear someone coming down the stairs…

Enter RUBY.

JILLIAN. Ruby. Look who's here!

RUBY. Fuck me. Joan.

JOAN. Well, hello, stranger!

RUBY. Fuck me. You look amazing.

JOAN. Thanks. I feel like someone Xeroxed me across the planet. But before they did they wiped their ass on me.

JILLIAN. Good gracious!

Enter GLORIA.

RUBY. My God, Joan. Your voice. It's amazing. And your skin! Seriously. How do you get your hair to do that?

JOAN *offers the flask.*

JOAN. Care to join us?

RUBY. Not many!

JILLIAN. It's Wild Turkey!

GLORIA. Is it now.

RUBY *drinks.*

RUBY. Woof. Gloria, you have to try this. That is something else. Deary me! Proper cowboy juice!

GLORIA. No thank you.

JOAN. Hello, Gloria.

Beat.

GLORIA. Joan. You'll have to forgive us, we were fast asleep.

JOAN. Well, it's late. Early. Who the fuck knows?

RUBY. That voice. I love it!

JILLIAN. Isn't it amazing!

RUBY. Here. Sorry about the heat. We're having a drought.

JOAN. Is it hot?

JILLIAN. She's used to it.

RUBY. Amazing. Like a lizard. A sexy lizard!

GLORIA. Yes. Perhaps you haven't heard about the drought
we're having. The rivers have dried up. The earth has turned
to stone. It's almost like it's a sign isn't it. I wonder… What
was the problem. With your travel arrangements.

RUBY. Say 'I'm the Bionic Woman'! Do Kojak! (*American
accent.*) 'Who loves ya baby!'

GLORIA. Yes, that voice? Is that your speaking voice?

JILLIAN. You mean the one she's speaking with.

RUBY (*American accent*). 'Who loves ya baby!'

JILLIAN. I was just saying wasn't I, Joan, I've just won
a pound off these two. They bet me you wouldn't make it.

GLORIA. Yes, Jillian. It turns out you were right and we were
wrong. Because lo and behold, here she is.

JOAN. Shit. I forgot. I brought gifts. Presents. Let's take a look
here… Okay.

She roots through her bag.

Jill, this is a Zippo and see? It's got the initials 'BK'
scratched in it. That's Bobby Keys. You know Bobby?

JILLIAN. Bobby Keys. I'm not sure –

JOAN. Bobby plays sax for The Rolling Stones. See. It works.

She lights it. Snaps it shut. Hands it to JILLIAN.

JILLIAN. Wow. (*Weakly hopeful.*) And you didn't even know
I smoked!

JOAN *takes a ring off her finger.*

JOAN. Ruby. This is a ring I was given by an Apache Shaman
in Big Sur. It's magic. You have to swap it round every
couple weeks or it turns your finger green.

RUBY. Gosh. It's beautiful.

JOAN. Wait till you see what I got you, Gloria. It's small but
just wait till you see it. I got it right here. It's a… where the
fuck is it.

She searches.

It was right here.

*She tips out the contents of her bag on the table and searches
through it.*

Okay. Just gimme a minute. It's here somewhere…

GLORIA (*tightly*). It's perfectly all right.

JOAN. Well. It's gone.

GLORIA (*flatly*). Has it.

JOAN. It was a harmonica. Leon Russell's harp. You know
Leon Russell, right?

GLORIA. No.

JOAN. You don't know Leon? Leon Russell is only the greatest
honky-tonk piano player in the world. Elton John stole his
entire act. He gave me his… A 1920s Marine Band, mother-
of-pearl inlay. I don't play harp. So I thought who do I know
who plays harp. The fuckin'… the harmonica? I know. My
sister Gloria.

Beat.

GLORIA. Well that's extremely thoughtful. Except I never
played harmonica.

Beat.

JOAN. Bullshit. You were always walking around with the…
Since you were, fucking…

GLORIA. No I wasn't.

JOAN. Am I going nuts?

GLORIA. Don't worry. But for the record, for your
information, I never played harmonica. Or 'harp'. I played –

She looks at JILLIAN.

I played the ukulele.

Beat.

JOAN. The ukulele?!

GLORIA. Yes, Joan.

JOAN. Well I'll be. Don't the memory play tricks?

Pause.

RUBY. So what have you been up to? Fill us in. We're all dying
to know.

JILLIAN. Golly. I mean… Where to start.

GLORIA. How about 1958?

RUBY. We got the album. Honest to God I've worn the grooves
out.

JILLIAN. That ballad.

RUBY. Heaven. The harmonies. Who is that? So so so so. Are
you are you – what? Are you planning others? A follow-up.
Albums. Platters. Any… any more in the pipeline?

GLORIA. That's a good question. Are there any more? Any
more albums on the way? Do you have a whatchamacallit.
Record deal, a contract? Or was it just the one?

Beat.

Also, are you planning to enquire after our mother's health at
any point?

Beat.

JOAN. Yeah... Look. I know this is a rough time for y'all.

JILLIAN. It is.

RUBY. Very, very rough. Very tough. It's been tough hasn't it?

JILLIAN. So tough. But now we're all here. But yes. It's been tough. A tough time.

GLORIA. But not for you?

Beat.

You said this is a tough time for *you*. Meaning us. Not you.

RUBY. Glor–

GLORIA. So I don't know if you know, Joan, but mother's cancer, her primary cancer, is stomach cancer. A tumour. This particular tumour can be caused by years and years of stress and worry, stress brought on by any number of things...

JILLIAN. Glor–

GLORIA. May I finish please, Jillian. I think it's important we fill Joan in so that we're all on the same page.

JOAN. Hey look I get it. Veronica's sick.

GLORIA. Stop. Hang about. Veronica. Who's Veronica?

RUBY. Okay –

GLORIA. What is it now. Twenty Christmases. No cards. No birthdays. Do you know I have two children? They're upstairs. Tony and Patty. They're out of nappies, through school and near as dammit out the other side.

JILLIAN. Are you blaming Joan for Mum being sick? Because if you are –

RUBY. Gloria.

JOAN. No it's okay.

Pause.

So, Gloria. First of all. Fuck off.

RUBY. Woof.

JILLIAN. Girls.

GLORIA. Charming. Very classy.

JOAN (*thick Blackpool accent*). Wanna play Knuckles? Chinese
    Burns? First one to squeal is a sissy for the summer.
    (*American.*) What happened, Gloria? As I remember – and
    let's face it – it's kinda hazy at this point – as I recall, one
    day we shared toys. Clothes. Hell, we even shared a room.
    The next it was like my face, voice, everything I did crawled
    clean up your little ass. Did something happen? I mean…
    Help me out here. Throw me a bone.

GLORIA (*mimics her voice*). 'Did something happen?'

    Beat.

    Aye, Joan. Something happened.

JOAN. Great. Because I'm dying to know.

JILLIAN. I told them. Last night. I told them what Mum told me.

RUBY. Okay, stop. Stop. Because you know what I think,
    sisters? I think, and you'll like this… Because I saw this
    sticker on the back a transit van coming out of the service
    station at Rochdale bypass, it said 'Today is the First Day of
    the Rest of Your Life'. (*Beat.*) Tomorrow. (*Beat.*) Today.
    '*Today* is the First Day'…

    And. Also. 'What Doesn't Kill You Makes You Stronger'.
    That's what they're saying. Someone on Nationwide said it
    and I thought –

    She mimes licking a pencil and writing it down.

    'That's good, I'll have that thank you very much.' I saw this
    other one, on this Cortina, it said 'SNOOPY FOR
    PRESIDENT'! It's good that int it. Snoopy! I mean… he's
    a dog! I absolutely adore young Charles Brown. Don't you
    just love him, Joan. Charlie Brown. Wait. Do you have him
    in America? What am I saying? Of course you do. Honestly,
    Joan! How on earth do you get your hair to do that? I've
    tried and tried. You just look fabulous. Like you've fallen out

the back of the telly. Off Charlie's Angels. Charlie Brown, Charlie's Angels. Listen to me! I've gone mad!

GLORIA. For God's sake, Ruby. Will you fuckin' pack it in?!

Silence.

Aye, Jillian told us. She told us the story. Is that why you went away? Is that why you went away and never came back. That's awfully sad. No it is. It's tragic. But see there's a problem. I was there. And I've got ears. (*Girly voice.*) 'I know a place we can go.' (*American man voice.*) 'Are you sure?' (*Girly.*) 'Mississippi.'

Beat.

'Just follow me, Mr Man. Come upstairs, and I'll show you Mississippi.'

Pause.

I watched you go in there. I listened at the door. 'What do you want?' 'I want to be a star.' 'Do ya, baby?' 'Oh please. Please, Mr Man, oh yes. Yes!…' (*With force.*) You killed us that night. And you killed Mum. And by the way, Mum wasn't even there. I was. And I saw. I saw everything.

Silence.

JOAN. Uhhhh… (*Shrugs.*) Okay.

Pause.

I mean, like I was saying to Jill here… I don't…

Pause.

But yeah. If you say so.

Pause.

JILLIAN. It's not true. Joan was fifteen. A man took her upstairs, with Mum's blessing –

JOAN. First of all, it was a long –

JILLIAN. – and he made you lie down / and you got pregnant.

JOAN (*overlapping*). It was a long / time ago.

JILLIAN (*overlapping*). Then she made you have an abortion.

JOAN. I've had lots of abortions.

GLORIA. See?

JILLIAN. It's true. Mum said.

GLORIA. 'Mum said.' Is this the same Mum drinks three bottles of sherry and dances up street in her frillies?

> *Beat.*

It's embarrassing this isn't it? These two prats. Sat by the door. Slavering, like whippets. 'Is that her? Oh please let it be!' 'I've been to Texas! California!' Jillian doesn't know any better, but Ruby? Seriously, do you honestly think in all these years you've spent wearing out one piss-poor LP, which no fucker bought – not my words – surviving on scraps, on Scotch mist, in all that time that she has spent five minutes thinking about you? (*To* JILLIAN.) Or you? Or me?

> *Beat.*

Being a mum isn't glamorous. It wears you out. You end up looking like me. Jillian has devoted her life to our mother. You may wish at some point to say thank you. Perhaps you're too upset. Perhaps you need to speak to your therapist. Perhaps when it's over, and you're back home, in your beach house, your penthouse, on your ranch, perhaps you'll wake up and write a song about it.

JILLIAN (*to* GLORIA). Have you finished? Because the doctor's on his way. (*To* JOAN.) She's in her room. Do you want me to come with you?

JOAN. No. It's okay.

JILLIAN. Now like I said, it's a bit of a shock, what with everything, but she'll absolutely one hundred percent know it's you. I know she will. I just know it.

> JOAN *looks at them all. She slowly walks to the stairs and looks up them.*

> *Pause.* JOAN *gazes up the stairs.*

GLORIA. Is there a problem, Joan?

Beat.

JILLIAN. Joan?

JOAN *looks up the stairs to see...*

YOUNG JOAN, *looking back down at her.*

GLORIA. Come on, pet! The doctor's on his way. Crack of dawn he said. Chop chop.

Pause.

JILLIAN. Joan... ?

JOAN *stands there. Looking at her younger self.*

Joan, I've spent years. Watching that woman. I've watched her shrivel and rot. You have to see her. You have to. She's your mum.

JOAN *gazes up the stairs.*

JOAN (*quietly*). Yes she is.

Pause.

JILLIAN. Joan?

Beat.

GLORIA. Come on lass. You've come all this way. Up you go.

Slowly, JOAN *turns from the stairs and walks back into the room.*

Desperate, JILLIAN *takes the photograph out of her dressing gown.*

JILLIAN. I found this. It's you and Mum, when it's just you. Look at it!

JOAN *doesn't.*

If you don't want to go up there you could write something on it, on the back, and I could read it out to her. Or just write your name.

GLORIA. Ha! An autograph?!

GLORIA *laughs bitterly.*

JILLIAN (*desperate*). Just go up there. Please. Joan. Please Joan. Please. Don't do this. Joan! For God's sake, forgive her! She's dying. Forgive her! Please. Forgive her!

JOAN *sits down on the bench. And lies down, like she did as a child. Smoking.*

GLORIA. What a washout. What a waste of an aeroplane ticket.

RUBY (*softly*). No.

GLORIA. Get up there and apologise.

RUBY. No. No, no, no, no, no...

GLORIA *stands over* JOAN. RUBY *backs into the corner.*

GLORIA. Apologise to that poor, poor woman. On your knees. You're good at that. It's straight up those stairs. Up the stairs and on your knees! Go on. DO IT! ON YOUR KNEES!

RUBY *starts to panic and sob.*

RUBY. Oh my God. Oh my God. Oh my God... OH MY GOD! OH MY GOD!!!

She breaks down, panicking.

JILLIAN. It's okay, Ruby. It's okay.

RUBY. I can't... I can't breathe!

JILLIAN. Breathe! Breathe Ruby!

RUBY. I can't. I can't... (*Gasps.*) What am I going to do? What am I going to do? You're Joan! What am I going to do? What's happening...

JILLIAN. It's all right. I'm here. I'm here.

RUBY. I can't go on! You're Joan! You're Joan! What did that man do to you?!

JILLIAN. Breathe!

RUBY. I can't! I can't! Where's Dennis? I want Dennis. I want Barry and Dennis.

JILLIAN. Ssshhhhh… It's all right. Jillian's here… Ssshhhhh. There there. Ssshhhhh.

As RUBY *recovers.*

GLORIA (*bitterly*). Well you know what they say, Ruby. Never meet your heroes.

JILLIAN *stands – finally snapping.*

JILLIAN. You know, Glor. This is perfect. It's just. You have, haven't you? You've seen your chance and you've pounced. What are you? You ghoul. Sharpening your fangs on the husk of your husband. My life's nothing, but at least I know it. I feel it every day. When did you last feel anything? You want Mum to notice you? To love you? Well it's too fucking late. And that's your fault. Not Joan's.

Beat.

Quietly, JOAN *speaks.*

JOAN. Damn. She's right.

She sits up.

Gloria, you're right.

It *was* a ukulele. I can see it.

And the piano *was* over there…

And there was flowers and candles and we danced on this table…

It's coming back! Well I'll be. I'll fuckin'. Flowers, candles. A ukulele!

JOAN *lights a cigarette.*

I'm not gonna lie. My recall's been wonky a while now. I'm out on the road, I'm sure the motel is right past the Texaco *then* left. Did they move it? Did they pick up the motel, the airport, and put it someplace else. Why do they keep moving shit around? Did Neil Young buy me a Scotch or tequila? Did that cowboy in Salinas smile at me first? They say everything happens for a reason. Bullshit. Bad things happen then good things happen. The donkey takes a dump. Roses grow. If you change one detail. If you're born a day later. If I'd put my right shoe on first. If if if if.

Beat.

If I didn't love Nat King Cole.

She stops. Looks at GLORIA.

You were a good kid, Gloria. Sang nice. Danced nice. (*Beat.*) Jill sang like a bird. Ruby sang and danced like an angel. But you. You were just. (*Beat.*) Don't get me wrong, you worked your ass off. But when the crunch came…

Beat.

And you knew it. Just like Mom did.

GLORIA *is very still.*

Beat.

It's like the song says. 'There's No People Like Show People'.

GLORIA *stands frozen.*

Ruby is show people. Jill is show people. You, Gloria. You are not show people.

Beat.

But if you want to go singing that song about how I fucked up your life, sure, I'll be in your song. I'll be 'Mack the Knife'. 'Mr Bojangles'. What was it Mom always said? 'A song is a place to be. Somewhere you can live.'

But don't go telling me what happened that night. You weren't there. Neither was Mom. The donkey takes a dump. Roses grow.

Beat.

Nobody killed your dreams, Gloria.

She looks up the stairs.

Just like nobody killed mine.

Beat.

It's been a hard road. What do I have to show for it, besides a few scars, keepsakes and eighty, ninety dollars, give or take.

Beat.

Should I throw in my cards? Maybe. Will I? Fuck no. I'm bound to this wheel for life. This is where I live and this is where I'll die. Like Mom. In a song.

GLORIA *is very still. The others too.*

All she wanted was for us to be safe.

Pause.

Do I blame her?

She shakes her head.

No.

Pause.

Can I go up there?

She shakes her head.

No.

Pause.

Why?

She looks up the stairs.

Because the girl who walked up those stairs never came back down.

Pause.

She's up there now.

Pause.

Holding her hand. Whispering in her ear.

Pause.

What she's saying… What she's saying only Mom knows.

Silence.

Enter the nurse, PENNY.

Pause.

PENNY. Hello there. I hope I'm not intruding.

JILLIAN. Penny.

Beat.

PENNY. I hope I'm not interrupting. It's just. There's somebody here…

Enter DR ROSE.

DR ROSE. Good morning. My name is Dr Rose.

JILLIAN. Good morning.

Pause.

Would you like a cup of tea?

DR ROSE. That's very kind. But I'm afraid I've a busy morning.

Silence.

JILLIAN. Right. Well.

Pause.

She's.

Beat.

She's upstairs.

Beat.

Shall I show you?

DR ROSE. Thank you.

JILLIAN. I'll show you.

PENNY. It's okay. I can do it. Then you can all be here together.

Beat.

It's warm out. And the sun's barely in the sky. It's going to be another lovely day.

Beat.

This way, doctor.

DR ROSE. Thank you. It's nice to meet you all.

PENNY *leads* DR ROSE *upstairs.*

Silence. Then –

JILLIAN. What am I going to do?

Pause.

JOAN (*softly*). Anything you want, Jill. (*Beat.*) Anything you want.

Pause.

Then... RUBY *asks softly...*

RUBY. Are there eagles?

Beat.

In California?

Pause.

And buzzards...

Pause.

JILLIAN. Is the ocean nice?

GLORIA *is very still.*

RUBY. Tell us about California. Something nice. Please.

JOAN *lights a cigarette.*

Pause.

JOAN. So recently I've been taking a small break from the fuckin'... the music. I moved out of my apartment to a smaller place, in a slightly cheaper, but perfectly lovely part of Los Angeles. And got myself a new table, and a new lamp, new cactus, and I said to myself look at that. This is a fresh start. But a girl has to eat, so I looked in the Yellow Pages and I found an agency, and I went for an interview and just like that I landed myself a job. A new apartment, table, lamp, job and cactus. All in one day.

JILLIAN. What is it you do?

JOAN. I deliver pizza. Giuseppe's Pizza.

> JOAN *goes to the piano. Tinkles some notes.*

Giuseppe's got twelve trucks, delivers all across Beverly Hills. Bel Air. They gave me a little yellow truck, and I drive out to the big houses, and I ring on the gates, and the gates open slowly, and I drive up and I smile and hand them the pizza. And they tip me a dollar. Sometimes two. Anyhow, few weeks back, I drive three Margheritas up to this big house in Stone Canyon and I ring on the gates, and I go inside, I walk up to the door and who's standing there?

JILLIAN. Who?

JOAN. Mrs Maxene Anglyn Andrews.

JILLIAN. Give over.

JOAN. Maxene Andrews, Jill. In the flesh. Sixty years old. Smoking a pink Sobranie in a long ivory holder, with a can of Budweiser beer. She can tell straight away I'm starstruck. We go inside, to her kitchen. There in the kitchen trying to open a bottle of wine, is Patty.

RUBY. Fuck off.

JOAN. Patty and Maxene Andrews. The two survivors. So I say something dumb like 'This is a beautiful house.' Patty doesn't even look up. 'This is what eighty million records buys you, honey.' They're alone in the house, so I ask, who's the third pizza for. Maxene says 'My schnauzer, Kitty.' And I look at her. And I look at Patty. And I burst into tears.

JILLIAN. No.

JOAN. I just… gush. And then…

RUBY. No.

JOAN. Then I tell them everything. Right from the beginning. About Mum and Joe Fogg, and the practices and the concerts, and they listen and Maxene looks at me and I see she has a tear in her eye. And I look at Patty and Patty does

too. Patty says 'Are you hungry?' And we take the wine and
the three pizzas, and we put them on this big white piano in
the conservatory. Patty says 'Where shall we start?' And
I say. 'How about "Pistol Packin' Mama".' Bang. Straight in.

(*Singing.*) Lay that pistol down, babe
Lay that pistol down

RUBY, JILLIAN *and* JOAN (*singing*).
Pistol packin' Mama
Lay that pistol down!

JILLIAN. Fuck me!

JOAN. We do the lot. 'Civilization'. 'Rumors are Flying'. 'Near
You'.

RUBY *and* JILLIAN. 'Boogie Woogie Bugle Boy'?!

JILLIAN. Give over!

JOAN. By the time we finished, the dog is asleep. The whole
case of wine is gone. Maxene and Patty are blotto, saying
they'll order pizza again tonight, tomorrow and every
night. I left at dawn, drove back to the store and Giuseppe
fired me.

JILLIAN. No!

JOAN. On the spot.

RUBY. So you never went back?

JOAN. Giuseppe took the truck back. I'd hike up, but those big
houses, they all look the same. Plus in Stone Canyon, they
have coyotes.

Pause.

RUBY. Is that a true story?

JOAN *smiles. She nods slowly.*

JOAN. It's a good one, right? A good story.

Pause.

GLORIA. 'They are four girls, and the Andrews are three. But
we've got one spare. In the wings. A spare wheel. Waiting. In
the background. And that girl's name… is Gloria.'

GLORIA*'s eyes fill with tears.*

Pause.

JOAN. At dawn, Patty turns to Maxene. 'Sisters, I'm tight as a drum. One more number. Pick a song, honey. "One for the road"'…

JOAN *goes to the piano and plays a couple of chords.*

(*Singing.*) Stars shining bright above you
Night breezes seem to whisper 'I love you' –

(*Spoken.*) Fuck! This is in tune!

(*Singing.*) Birds singin' in the sycamore tree –

JILLIAN *and* JOAN (*singing*).
Dream a little dream of me

JOAN (*singing*). Say 'nighty-night' and kiss me –

JILLIAN, JOAN *and* RUBY (*singing*).
Just hold me tight and tell me you'll miss me
While I'm alone and blue as can be –

RUBY. Did I go up there?

JILLIAN. You went down.

RUBY. Are you sure? Hang about.

(*Singing.*) While I'm alone and blue as can be –

JILLIAN, JOAN *and* RUBY (*singing*).
Dream a little dream of me

GLORIA (*singing*).
Stars fading but I linger on, dear
Still craving your kiss –

ALL FOUR (*singing*).
I'm longing to linger till dawn, dear
Just saying this –

JILLIAN. That's it.

RUBY. I'm wobbling.

ALL FOUR (*singing*).
Sweet dreams till sunbeams find you
Sweet dreams that leave all worries behind you
But in your dreams, whatever they be
Dream a little dream of me

RUBY (*calling*). How's that, Mum?!

The YOUNG WEBB SISTERS *appear and sing.*

YOUNG SISTERS (*singing*).
Stars shining bright above you
Night breezes seem to whisper 'I love you'
Birds singin' in the sycamore tree
Dream a little dream of me

As they sing, JOAN *fetches her coat and leaves.*

Say 'nighty-night' and kiss me
Just hold me tight and tell me you'll miss me
While I'm alone and blue as can be
Dream a little dream of me

Stars fading but I linger on, dear
Still craving your kiss
I'm longing to linger till dawn, dear
Just saying this –

YOUNG JOAN (*singing*).
Sweet dreams till sunbeams find you
Sweet dreams that leave all worries behind you
But in your dreams, whatever they be –

Blackout.

The End.

JEZ BUTTERWORTH

Jez Butterworth was born in London in 1969 and studied English at St John's College, Cambridge.

His first play, *Mojo* (Royal Court Theatre, 1995), won seven major awards, including the Olivier Award for Best Comedy. Other plays include *The Night Heron* (2002), *The Winterling* (2006), *Parlour Song* (2008), *Jerusalem* (2009), *The River* (2012) and *The Ferryman* (2017).

Jerusalem transferred from the Royal Court to the West End, breaking box-office records for a new play. It won Best Play at the Evening Standard Awards 2010, the UK Critics' Circle Award for Best Play 2010, before travelling to Broadway where it won Best Foreign Play, at the New York Critics' Circle Awards 2011. It received six Tony nominations, winning two, including Best Actor for Mark Rylance. *The River* transferred to Broadway in 2014, starring Hugh Jackman.

His sixth play for the Royal Court, *The Ferryman*, directed by Sam Mendes, was extended during its transfer to the West End. It received fifteen five-star reviews in the UK daily press and won Best Play and Best Director at the Evening Standard Theatre Awards in 2017, the Critics' Circle Award for Best Play, and three Olivier Awards for Best Play, Best Director and Best Actress in 2018. In 2018, *The Ferryman* transferred to Broadway and was nominated for nine Tony Awards, winning four including the award for Best Play 2019.

Jez's screenwriting credits include *Fair Game* (2010) directed by Doug Liman and starring Sean Penn and Naomi Watts, *Get On Up* (2014) directed by Tate Taylor and starring Chadwick Boseman and Octavia Spencer, *Edge of Tomorrow* (2014) directed by Doug Liman and starring Tom Cruise and Emily Blunt, *Black Mass* (2015) directed by Scott Cooper and starring Johnny Depp and Dakota Johnson, *Spectre* (2015) directed by Sam Mendes and starring Daniel Craig and Naomie Harris, *Ford v Ferrari* (2019) directed by James Mangold and starring Matt Damon and Christian Bale, *Indiana Jones and the Dial of Destiny* (2023) directed by James Mangold and starring Harrison Ford, Antonio Banderas and Phoebe Waller-Bridge.

For TV, Jez has created and written the comedy series *Mammals* for Amazon Studios starring James Corden, Sally Hawkins, Melia Kreiling and Colin Morgan. Jez also created the historical fantasy drama *Britannia* which was the first co-production between Sky and Amazon Prime. It stars David Morrissey, Zoë Wanamaker and Mackenzie Crook and ran for three seasons.

In 2007, Jez won the E. M. Forster Award from the American Academy of Arts and Letters. In 2019 he was elected as a Fellow of the Royal Society of Literature.